# Fishing Spirit Lake

Copyright © 2014 Ted L. Estess
All Rights Reserved
Manufactured in the United States

ISBN: 978-0-9915321-0-0
Library of Congress Control Number: 2014948285
Cover Art: Albert Bierstadt, details from "Mount Corcoran"
Book Design: Theresa Ener

Lamar University Press
Beaumont, TX

# Acknowledgments

I am grateful to the editors of the following journals and anthologies for publishing chapters of this book.

*Concho River Review*
*Disturbances in the Field*
*El Paso Review*
*Honors in Practice*
*Image: A Journal of the Arts & Religion*
*In a Field of Green*
*Journal of the National Collegiate Honors Council*
*Windhover*

From Lamar University Press

Jean Andrews, *High Tides, Low Tides: the Story of Leroy Colombo*
Robert Murray Davis, *Levels of Incompetence: An Academic Life*
Gerald Duff, *Memphis Mojo*
Dominique Inge, *A Garden on the Brazos*
Gretchen Johnson, *The Joy of Deception and Other Stories*
Christopher Linforth, *When You Find Us We Will Be Gone*
Tom Mack and Andrew Geyer, eds, *A Shared Voice*
Harold Raley, *Louisiana Rogue*
Jim Sanderson, *Trashy Behavior*
Jan Seale, *Appearances*
Melvin Sterne. *The Number You Have Reached*
Robert Wexelblatt, *The Artist Wears Rough Clothing*

For more information on these and other books, go to
www.LamarUniversityPress.Org


Also by Ted L. Estess:
*Elie Wiesel*
*Be Well: Reflections on Graduating from College*
*The Cream Pitcher: Mississippi Stories*

For Sybil and Barrett

# CONTENTS

| | |
|---|---|
| 1 | My Life as a Laputan |
| 13 | You're Not God |
| 25 | A Ball in a Box |
| 33 | Bounded Grace |
| 45 | Mint Juleps in January |
| 55 | A Picture Holds Us Captive |
| 67 | The Importunate Giver |
| 77 | Montana State of Mind |
| 89 | The Day I Flew in A Canoe |
| 97 | We're Having a Baby |
| 109 | La Leche |
| 117 | Fishing Spirit Lake |
| 127 | Losing What You Love and Getting It Back Again |
| 143 | A Fishing Medley |
| 153 | Becoming Part of A Story |
| 163 | The Point of Fishing |
| 173 | Catch and Release |

After the crack-up comes the grateful rush into ordinary life.
—Philip Roth


As swimmers dare
to lie face to the sky
and water bears them,
as hawks rest upon air
and air sustains them,
so would I learn to attain
freefall, and float
into Creator Spirit's deep embrace,
knowing no effort earns
that all-surrounding grace.
—Denise Levertov

# My Life as a Laputan

Soon after 9 p.m., I climbed aboard a Continental Trailways bus and stared through green glass as my parents watched the second of their two sons head off to college. Leaving the station, the bus moved into the bayous of south Louisiana along old Highway 90, then over the swamps and across rice and sugar cane fields, and on through a night of small towns, finally climbing the Sabine River bridge into Texas, where a mileage marker announced *New Mexico 878 miles*. That should give any young man room enough.

The bus stopped at 5 a.m. at a larger Trailways station where I was to get the seven o'clock to Waco. After a modest breakfast, I examined the racks of paperback books, thinking this the proper thing for an aspiring young scholar to do. I overcame my shyness to make two purchases: Dale Carnegie's *How to Win Friends and Influence People* and another august volume, author unknown, entitled *Sex and the Adolescent*.

Bought for fifty cents each in the Trailways bus station in Houston, Texas, the two new books doubled the size of the library that I was taking to college. Stowed in my trunk in the belly of the bus was a Webster's dictionary that had lain, largely unused, around the house for thirty years; and in a black plastic folder at my side was a King James Bible, red letter edition, a leather-bound high school graduation gift with my name embossed in gold on its flexible cover.

There were not many books in my house in Tylertown, Mississippi. My parents prized education but didn't buy books. But, as I was soon to learn, I had somehow managed to read about as many books as most of my Baylor University classmates, which in the fall of 1960 was not saying a great deal.

Settled back into the Trailways seat, I glanced first at Carnegie, who, I quickly concluded, had nothing whatsoever to teach me about winning friends and influencing people. Whatever deficiencies I was carrying to the

Ted L. Estess

halls of academe, I was not lacking the capacities requisite to endearing myself to others. All you have to do is say *Hello* and ask a question or two, and people will take you to be a lodestone of generosity and goodwill. Sit me down by a stranger on a bus bound for any place, and, in no time, I'll win a friend and influence a people.

Sex is another matter. So it was from a state of some wonder that I expectantly turned the pages of *Sex and the Adolescent* as the Trailways moved through Waller and Hempstead, deep into the heart of Texas. A curious woman in the seat opposite leaned over to see what I was reading, but I shielded the book from her. It was my first day in Texas, and I didn't want to ruin my reputation.

When I stepped out of the yellow cab and stood for the first time in front of Kokernot Hall on the campus of Baylor University, I could not foresee that four years hence I would drive away from that place, alone in my first car, a '58 black Custom Ford with overdrive, and that there they would be—on the seats and in the trunk, surrounding the spare tire and in the glove compartment, stuffed in every crevice—hundreds of them, books, books, books on every subject, but especially novels and plays and poetry, theology and philosophy, history and comparative religion.

Neither could I foresee that four years hence I would have read nigh all of William Faulkner, and would have spent days with King Lear, and would have found that I could not understand philosophers named Duns Scotus and William of Ockham, and would been kept alive by a theologian named Paul Tillich and a storyteller named Eudora Welty, and that I would have taken a liking to Eastern stuff, would even have fancied myself becoming a Zen Buddhist and meditating for fourteen hours a day.

When I drove out of Texas in the summer of 1964, I could not then foresee that four years later, in 1968, I would drive away again, this time from Louisville, Kentucky, and this time with a beautiful young wife named Sybil, who by then would have taught me considerably more than I could ever have hoped to learn from that slender volume I purchased in 1960 in the Trailways station in Houston, Texas, and it wasn't about winning friends and influencing people either.

But when we drove away from Kentucky in 1968, our new, baby-blue Chevy Nova couldn't hold them all. I had to call up Mayflower. It was with some pride that I responded to the fellow who was loading the dozens of boxes onto that moving van when he said to me, "Son, you got more books than any man I ever seed. Whut-chu do wid all dez books?"

"I read 'em, Sir."

"Son, don't mess wid me. Ain't no man gonna read dat many books." As if to give me fair warning, he added, "He'd better not."

Arriving at Syracuse University, I wasn't sure why my teacher in Kentucky had told me to go north to study. Maybe he thought it would be good for me to meet people who were not like me, to encounter, as we say now in the university, *difference*, and to meet people who didn't know as much as I about winning friends and influencing people.

To tell the truth, during those first years in Syracuse, I tried to erase the differences between me and the people whom I was meeting. I tried to disguise where I had come from. I fiercely smoked my pipe and tried to talk right, a feckless project that I had begun back in Kentucky. I had bought my first pipe from a store on 4th Street in Louisville. My philosophy teacher there, an Englishman named Eric Rust, had studied at Oxford and had read everything I wanted to read, and he smoked a pipe. He also talked right. I went out to his house one day and we discussed my paper on Tillich. Surrounded by books in several languages and sitting in a room filled with the incense of sweet tobacco, he was just the kind of man I wanted to be. All I needed to do was to buy a pipe, read lots of books, and change the way I talked. That seemed easy enough to do.

So I took that pipe and sat out under the great maple tree that shaded Sybil's and my balcony at our apartment in a grand old house on South Peterson Street. There I sat, day after day, month after month, reading books and smoking my pipe. One nice thing about a pipe is that you can spend the best part of an afternoon just trying to light the thing.

After a year or two, I got pretty good at smoking that pipe, and I read a lot more books, but I still didn't talk right. I tried to remember to add *g* to words like *talking*, *fixing*, and *reading*. So instead of saying, "I wuz talkin' to my teacher, and I told him I wuz fixin' to do sum readin' this summer," I tried real hard to say, "I wuz talk-ING to my teacher, and I told him I wuz fix-ING to do sum read-ING this summer."

Talking right is one of the hardest things I ever tried to do. Living in Syracuse, New York, was a benefit in that regard, because everybody in Syracuse talked right, except Sybil and me, and we were trying to. After a few weeks there, I stopped saying *thang* and *Fridee*, and started saying *thing* and *Friday*. It's amazing how much better you feel when you talk right.

I was doing pretty well until one night in Atlanta, Georgia. I was there for a conference, and I met a linguist who taught at the University of Hawaii. We were visiting at a reception after a lecture by Tom Altizer, who was one of those death-of-God theologians popular at the time. Back then, I thought it worth the trouble to travel all the way from Syracuse, New York, to Atlanta, Georgia, to spend a couple of days talking about the subject. That Hawaiian linguist and I got to talking, and I thought I was sounding pretty good when she stopped right in the middle of the conversation and asked, "Where in the world are you from?"

"Well, originally I'm from Mississippi," I mumbled. As I always did in those years, I said I was *originally* from Mississippi to show that I had come up in the world. But I quickly added, "I've lived four years in Texas, four in Kentucky, and a couple in Syracuse, New York," speaking more clearly the further north I went on the list.

"Well, you really have messed up the way you talk," she said. "You speak with a little of this accent and a little of that accent. It's very unpleasant to listen to. I think you should talk like people talk in Mississippi. It's a beautiful way to talk."

I didn't hear anything else she said the rest of the night. Here I had bought a pipe and was getting along toward talking right and this little woman from Hawaii was suggesting I was on the wrong track. She probably wouldn't have liked my pipe either, but I didn't tell her about that.

Perhaps, then, I needed to go north not to encounter something different, but in order to see myself as different and to see the place I had come from as different, maybe special. Getting away from my own place, perhaps I would be able to see it as the place it is, myself as well.

But, frankly, I went to Syracuse, New York, trying hard to become something else. Whatever I was, was not enough. Perhaps it was not even good. I didn't talk right and everybody on TV seemed to think that my kind of folks lynched Black folks and were ignorant. They didn't associate me with William Faulkner, Eudora Welty, or even Willie Morris, but with Ross Barnett, George Wallace, and Bull Connor.

"Do you know any people who kill Negroes?" a woman asked me one day at a gift shop in Cazenovia, New York. I was browsing and she was making small talk with a stranger. She first asked where my accent came from. I admitted that originally I am from Mississippi. She asked her next question to make conversation. It just popped in her mind. No insult intended. "Do you know any people who kill Negroes?"

I felt accused and guilty and didn't know what to say. I said, "Not more than two or three hundred." I walked out, feeling worse for having gone to Cazenovia on a beautiful spring day.

But as is often the case, you don't really know why you go to a place until you've been there for a while. You go for one reason, only later to discover the real reason.

The real reason—at least one of the real reasons—I went to Syracuse, New York, was to become a Mississippian. In the Deep North, there was nothing else for me to be.

All this reminds me of the trips that Sybil and I made to Mississippi from Syracuse. Whenever we got back to Syracuse after a couple of weeks in Mississippi, folks would want to have us over for dinner. I thought this was mighty nice until I began to think that perhaps our hosts wanted not so much to see Sybil and me, but to hear us talk about Mississippi. They wanted to see us *because* we had been to Mississippi and had returned, which at the time seemed unlikely for a lot of folks living in Syracuse, New York. To them, Mississippi wasn't Pluto, but it was in the neighborhood.

Take our friends Tom and Ellen Ewens. They would plan for weeks to have Sybil and me to dinner as soon as we got back from a few weeks in the South. Tom would lay in plenty of food and drink and put on a fine meal. For two or three hours, Sybil and I would tell Mississippi stories, and Tom and Ellen would listen as though we had just arrived from outer space.

"Tom," I said one night, trotting out my best Mississippi drawl, "Sybil and I wuz coming up from Poplarville the other day, and we decided to stay off the Interstate and come up on old Highway 11."

"Is dat the same Highway 11 dat cums to Syracuse," Tom asked, trying himself to talk with a proper Southern accent, but he should have known a man from Wisconsin *cain't* talk *rite*.

"The very one," I said. "It starts in Nawleens and goes right through Poplarville, not a hundred yards from the house Sybil grew up in. You know, they named Poplarville after a fellow named 'Poplar' Jim Smith. Well, anyway, we wuz moseying along on Highway 11, and got up above Nashville, Tennessee, headed toward Bristol and Kingsport, and it wuz getting along toward dark, and we wuz getting worried about finding a place to stay. So I stopped at this run-down garage to ask if there wuz any places to stay at on up toward Bristol. 'Howdy,' I said to the mechanic in the garage. 'I'm driving north on Highway 11. Can I get a place to stay at on up the road?'"

"Why, man," the mechanic replied, "that-air road runs die-rek to New York City. You can git a place to stay at wherever you wants to on that-air road."

At that, Tom and Ellen Ewens fell out laughing.

Now, you tell me, why would my friend Tom Ewens and his wife Ellen, he from Wisconsin, a philosopher and a psychoanalyst, and she an accomplished Montessori teacher from Rhode Island, nigh split their sides laughing when I told them that story? It's not all that funny. Tom got up to get something else for the table, repeating the very words to himself as he walked to the kitchen, "Why, man, that-air road runs die-rek to New York City." He went on laughing just to hear the words, "That-air road runs die-rek to New York City." What I didn't tell that man in Tennessee is that Highway 11 doesn't run direct to New York City. It stays west and eventually goes, as Tom had wondered, right into the heart of Syracuse, New York, which was why I was driving on it in the first place.

Perhaps the real reason I went to Syracuse was to meet Tom and Ellen Ewens, and obviously I couldn't have known that before I went. Meeting them did not make me something else, but it did change me. In retrospect, I see that it made me more truly what I am. At least I started paying attention to my place and people. For me, it was going north toward home.

It reminds me of an Hasidic story. Rebbe Zusia once said, "When I die, the Celestial Judge will not ask why I was not Abraham or Isaac or Jacob. The Celestial Judge will ask why I was not Zusia."

But I didn't go to Syracuse, New York, with all that in mind. I went to do serious research in religion and literature. To tell the truth, being serious was more important than religion and literature. They were only the vehicles by which I exercised what was most important: my seriousness.

Perhaps that is why Steve Langfur and I became good friends. Like me, Langfur had a terminal case of seriousness. He looked like a refugee from a Bergman movie or a Beckett play, gaunt and somber, dark and isolated. He was a man floating alone on an iceberg in the middle of the North Sea. Repeatedly, he narrowed his eyes, which were hardly visible beneath his black, bushy eyebrows. He was a philosopher on leave from the *Schwartzwald*—the Black Forest—and he was overdosing on Martin Heidegger's *Being and Time—Sein und Zeit*.

Later, my friend interrupted his graduate study and took his new wife, a Sabra from Israel and a bundle of Middle Eastern passion if there ever was one, up to a Vermont mountain shack and stashed himself away to read nothing but Martin Heidegger. *Sorge*—concern, care—that was one of Heidegger's big words. Langfur was full of *Sorge*, serious *Sorge*, ultimate *Sorge*, as Paul Tillich would have it.

So was I: full of it. It was hard to tell which of us was the fuller of it. Langfur's German was better than mine, but I was as full of *Sorge*.

Back then I had the idea that in order to say much of anything about a thinker I needed to read everything he or she had written. Not a bad plan for an eager young scholar, I suppose, but such a plan ill fits a man for ordinary life. You don't have time to take out the garbage or be a decent husband or vote if you set about to read—as I did—all of Paul Tillich, Martin Heidegger, Samuel Beckett, William Faulkner, Emily Dickinson, Wallace Stevens, and many other lights, including W. H. Auden, Harold Pinter, Jean Genet, Albert Camus, Eugene Ionesco, Eugene O'Neill, John Updike, James Baldwin, Joseph Heller, Tennessee Williams, Ralph Ellison, William Styron, Philip Wheelwright, Suzanne Langer, Hannah Arendt, Norman O. Brown, and Herbert Marcuse, with Nietzsche, Freud, and Marx thrown in for good measure. And that is not to mention the Bible, Luther, Augustine, Schleiermacher, and, the best of the lot, Miss Eudora Welty.

What surprises me now is not that I was captive to such a program of study, but that I was so successful, if that is the word, in following it. But I couldn't keep it up.

Looking back, I see that I made a fundamental mistake with regard to books. For one thing, I read too many. In that, I wasn't much different from most eager young scholars who get hooked on books. Even Voltaire said he read too many books, Nietzsche, too.

Now I'm all for reading. I spend the best part of my waking hours cajoling students to read books, and I still read a fair number myself. But too many books can pretty near ruin a man, or a woman for that matter.

Some people suggest that women are somehow inoculated against the mischief that too many books can cause. They say that women are less inclined to abstraction, that they are more connected with others and more, as they say, *relational* in their way of thinking and living. I don't know about all that, but I do know that too many books can ruin a good woman as fast as they can a good man. Women, as well as men, can miss their own lives.

Too many books—at least too many books read in the wrong way—can distance a person from ordinary life. Books can take you clean out of the space and time of your own life. After ten or twelve years of doing little more than reading books, you will hardly know where you are and will barely know the time of day.

Take Langfur. After two years in a shack on the side of a Vermont mountain with nothing for company except his puzzled wife, a potbellied stove, and a stack of books by Martin Heidegger, in German, too, he couldn't find his way around a city block. A few years later, he moved to Israel trying to help his wife recover her sanity. He wrote me that he had discovered his element. He said his element was the sun.

That's what locking yourself up in a shack in Vermont and reading Martin Heidegger for two years will do to you: you'll be thirty-five years old before you notice the sun.

But reading too many books was only part of the problem. I read books in the wrong way. I thought that reading books is like climbing Mount Ida. Mount Ida is a 12,000-foot peak just north of where Sybil and I spend time in the summer in Colorado. When I am out there, I sometimes think I might climb Mount Ida one day. I could drive about ten miles up the road, hike up Timber Lake trail, and after five hours or so, I would be at the summit of Mount Ida. It would be a strenuous walk, but possible even for a man in my kind of shape.

In Syracuse, I thought that reading Paul Tillich, or anyone else, was like climbing Mount Ida. You get on the trail; walk up the slope; reach the summit; smoke your pipe; and come back down. Then you move on to another mountain. There are always more peaks in the distance. They are like scoops of ice cream on an infinitely high cone.

But reading Paul Tillich or William Faulkner or Emily Dickinson is not like climbing Mount Ida. Doing x-ray crystallography or working out a computer-aided design are, in important ways, not like climbing Mount Ida either.

Coming to know things that are really important is like coming to know a face. There is no summit to a face. You cannot conquer a face. I can never say I am finished and done with Sybil's face. It changes day to day, hence my knowing of her is always partial, incomplete, provisional. My teacher Stanley Hopper, following Nietzsche, would call my knowing of her *perspectival*.

Now my teachers Stanley Hopper and David Miller could have taught me all this; and when I was in Syracuse, they probably tried. If they did, I missed it. But, in fact, I was doing precisely what they had done. They too had worked, and nearly succeeded, at reading nigh every book that had been written in about five fields, theology, psychology, philosophy, literature, mythology, and the like. When I was studying with them, they added Eastern texts to the list; so I smoked my pipe and read the *Dhammapada*, the *Rig Veda*, the *Tao te Ching*, and the *Analects of Confucius*. You can add the *Bhagavad-Gita* and parts of the *Upanishads* as well.

My mind was like a garbage can. I was tossing everything in as fast as possible. It's a wonder I got out with an ounce of sanity left. Sybil says I didn't.

I tell you what I was. I was a Laputan. You remember the Laputans. They are those folks who live on that floating island called Laputa in *Gulliver's Travels*. The Laputans are so taken up with speculation that they are like their island home, floating above reality. In fact, they are so engrossed in thought that they forget where they are; and if they are not careful, they'll fall in a hole or walk right off the island. Gulliver says that they can neither speak nor hear the speech of others "without being roused by some external taction upon [their] organs of speech and hearing."

The Laputans need help from a Flapper. The Flapper holds a stick to which is attached a slightly inflated balloon filled with peas or pebbles. When the Laputan falls dangerously deep into thought, the Flapper takes the balloon—made from the bladder of a sheep—and flaps it against the eyes and ears of the Laputan. The Flapper brings the Laputan out of thought and back to his senses. For a while, the Laputan recovers himself in the space and time of his own life.

For a few years in Syracuse, New York, I was a Laputan and Sybil was my Flapper. Unless she roused my organs of speech and hearing with some external tactions, I was mostly as deaf and dumb as a fence post.

Perhaps that was why my teacher in Kentucky told me to go north to study: he knew I needed to learn to pay attention to things right before my eyes—to learn more fully to inhabit the spaces and times of my own life.

To tell you the truth, I've spent the best part of my life unlearning a good deal of what my teachers taught me, but maybe that's the way it always is between good teachers and their students. A teacher teaches and the student learns; and then the student must unlearn what the teacher taught in order to teach someone else.

Is it necessarily the case that we must spend a good part of our life recovering from our education?

One afternoon I went out to Professor Hopper's house for a little conversation about Martin Heidegger. It was an oral exam. I was not up to Heidegger, but I had schlepped up the mountain and was ready to expound on his concepts of *Da sein, Geschichte, gegenwürtigen, existenzial,* and *existenziel.* Hopper favored the later Heidegger, so I was ready to talk about poetry and the poet's special capacity to step into the clearing of being and to make present what Heidegger calls the four-fold—mortals, the earth, the sun, the gods. *That which you seek is near and is already coming to meet you.* I was ready to quote that line from Hölderlin if need be, but I didn't know whether he wrote it before or after he went mad.

Professor Hopper met me at the door, dressed, as always, in a gray suit, white shirt, and tie. We were downstairs, and there they were, everywhere. I stared at them. Books, books, books, thousands and thousands of books, covering the walls from floor to ceiling in three large basement rooms, and that was only part of his library. I stared and wanted to run out the door and go away to a shack in Vermont and smoke my pipe and read some more books before taking that exam. "Ted," Dr. Hopper asked, "would you like a cup of tea before we talk about Heidegger?"

"That would be fine, Dr. Hopper," I said. We got to the kitchen, and my genial teacher started opening cabinet doors one after the other. He reminded me of Mr. Magoo looking for his glasses.

"Now where does Helen keep the tea? Let me see. Ted, where would you suppose that Helen keeps the tea?"

"I don't know, Dr. Hopper. Maybe there above the oven, in that cabinet there."

"Ted, you're right. Here's the tea. Now, Ted," Professor Hopper asked, "how did you know that Helen keeps the tea above the oven?"

"I don't know, Dr. Hopper. That's where Sybil and I keep the tea at our house, I guess."

"Well, Ted, where do you think Helen keeps the kettle?"

"It's there, Dr. Hopper, there on the stove."

The reluctant light of the Syracuse winter came through the living room windows, and we talked about Martin Heidegger and poetry and about the death and rebirth of the gods. "It is the time of the god that is no more and the not yet of the gods that are to come," I said, quoting Heidegger who was writing of Hölderlin.

"I think so, Ted," Professor Hopper said. "It's like what Wallace Stevens says, 'We live in a new dispensation of the sun.' But to step into that new dispensation, we must first step back, and then down. Then we must 'step barefoot into reality.'"

"That reminds me," Professor Hopper added, "of the story that Nishitani Sensei told me when I saw him in Kyoto. You know the story. The student goes to the Master and asks, 'How can I be enlightened?' The Master offers him a cup of tea and starts to pour. And the student impatiently asks again, 'Master, how can I be enlightened?' All the time, the Master is pouring tea. The tea starts to overflow the cup. It runs out on the tatami mat. Finally, the student interrupts. 'Master,' he says, 'the tea is overflowing the cup.' The Master replies, 'You must first empty the cup before it can be filled.'"

"There's Helen," Professor Hopper exclaimed. "Helen, Helen. Ted's here. Come, Helen, and say hello to Ted."

It was good to see Helen, this former church organist now displaying the first signs of what was to become severe Parkinson's. "Helen," Dr. Hopper said, "Ted had to help me find the tea. I couldn't lay my hands on the tea, Helen."

"I'm not surprised, Stanley," Helen replied. "I'm really not surprised."

Professor Hopper said I did okay on the exam, but I doubted it. I wasn't sure anything I was seeking was coming near.

When I got to our apartment that afternoon, I sat down with my pipe and my well-worn copy of *Being and Time* to check some things that had come up in the exam. Somehow my effort to be in time seemed all but futile.

The dark sky of the Syracuse afternoon had invaded the room; so I put Heidegger and my pipe aside and wandered into the kitchen. It was a clean, well-lighted room. I poured some of the dark, redolent Columbian beans into the coffee grinder. I was surprised again at how much noise a coffee grinder makes and at how good freshly ground coffee smells. I got the water boiling and the kettle whistling and fitted a filter into the carafe and poured steaming water across the coffee. I watched the grounds soak up the water and heard the *slinpk, slinpk* against the glass. I got out our best china. When I heard the car crunch the snow on the driveway, I poured two cups of fine coffee. With sugar and cream and napkins on the tray, I went to the living room just as Sybil came in from work.

"Here, Honey, I thought you might like some coffee after a long day."

"Ted, that coffee smells delicious. This is the nicest thing that's happened to me all day."

## You're Not God

I had no way of knowing it at the time, but growing up in a small, county seat town in South Mississippi did have advantages. After all, you didn't have to be much of anybody to be somebody in a town of 1200 people in South Mississippi in the 1950s. Growing a big tomato could get a farmer's picture in the weekly newspaper.

And though I maintained an "aw-shucks-it's-not-much" attitude, I had my picture in the paper lots of times. Little wonder, then, that when I got on that bus in the fall of 1960, I had hardly a shred of self-doubt or apprehension. I hadn't yet heard of what John Keats calls "negative capability"—by which he means the capacity, as he says, "of being in uncertainties, Mysteries, doubts without any irritable reaching after fact and reason." As that bus wended its way across the great expanse of Louisiana swamp into Texas, I very much needed that capacity, but had no way of knowing it. I wanted certainty and answers, not doubt and mysteries.

My first English course did as much as anything to deflate my uninformed self-confidence. I can't recall her name, but she terrorized a hundred-and-twenty freshman during that long fall of 1960. She smiled, commiserated, and flunked us. At the end of the class, she congratulated me for getting a B, the first in my life. She said that had I not misspelled a word in my last essay I would have done better. I later learned she had not given a single one A. Not one in one-hundred-twenty students measured up.

Music theory gave me more of the same. At the end of the fall semester Professor Frank Smith suggested that my friend Judith McCleary and I move up to the honors section in the spring. Unknowingly, Frank Smith settled my fate. Had I stayed in his class, my musical deficiencies might have remained hidden, and I might well have remained on the path of becoming an organist-choir master. After all, I had been the best pianist in Tylertown, Mississippi, and the organist at the Baptist Church. That should count for something.

The teacher was a madman named Nicholas England. Over the years I've realized that this is one good reason to go to college: young people need to undergo the tutelage of monomaniacs and attempt to scale the expectations of persons who have dedicated decades to studying a single problem or acquiring a specific art, obsessively so. Martha Graham knew what I am talking about when she asked, "How many leaps did Nijinsky take before he took the one that startled the world?" Nijinsky, of course, took thousands and thousands of leaps before he took the leap that startled the world.

My particular maniac had gone off to Cornell and gotten interested in East African tribal music. He had come to Baylor University determined to introduce young Baptist hymn singers to the rhythmical intricacies native to the jungles and bush of East Africa. For much of my life to that point, I had thought syncopation the first step on the slippery slope to fornication. Nothing off-beat for me, thank you. I could follow a pattern, an unwavering beat, but was lost when things got more complicated whether at the keyboard or between bodies.

Nicholas England knew all that, and he wanted to change it. The first day he said to the class, "Start this rhythm with your right hand," and we started marking the time on our desks. Then he said, "Keep it going and add this with your left hand," and he introduced a counter-rhythm, not a simple syncopation, but something radical, or so it seemed to me. He had something like a 3-beat going against an 8 or some god-knows what jungle pattern. I kept my right hand bobbing and my left hand pumping, all the time maintaining on my face a look of intense concentration moderated with a slight smile, as if to say, "I'm really into this, Dr. England."

I was lost, and I knew it. Only the second semester of college and I was a dead man.

About a month into the semester, England proposed a deal: he was the stage manager for the spring production of *Peter Grimes*, and he said that anyone who helped build the set for the opera would have his grade upped one letter for the semester. He was lying, but I was desperate.

There was this guy in the class that everyone called Pudgy Smith from Fort Worth. Pudgy didn't need to help build England's set: he was a musical genius. But I was there at 2 o'clock every Friday afternoon, eager to show England that if I could not bi-dexterously produce jungle rhythms, I could handle a saw and hammer with the best of them. England was not impressed. Only rhythm impressed him, and I had the rhythm of a toad frog.

We came to the final exam, and there sat Pudgy Smith from Fort Worth. I despised him. He had perfect pitch. I had mediocre relative pitch. Pudgy's piano technique was brilliant. Mine was behind schedule. England praised him. He ignored me.

I managed the harmonization all right. After all, you can get by in harmonization by following the rules, and I could follow rules. Then came sight singing.

The warming breeze of early May wafted through the open windows. I sat frozen, terrified, awaiting my turn. England passed from student to student, gazing down from his six-foot-five-inch frame to indicate, "Next." He came to me, handed me a sheet of music, and gave the pitch to start. For two miserable minutes I sang, or bayed, tones of such consummate ugliness that Pudgy Smith and Nicholas England and eleven other Honors students listened in stricken awe: never had they been subjected to such piteous sounds of fear and desperation.

Next came musical dictation. England sat at the piano and said he would play the selection two times and we would write down what he had played. For Professor Smith the previous semester, I had done okay with dictation, but he had stayed within manageable melodies and expected harmonics, and he had played the selection three times. Nicholas ranged over four octaves, employing intricate harmonies and developing a complex melody and using mystifying rhythms. You would have thought he was debuting at Carnegie hall. The music stopped. Silence fell heavy upon the room.

One classmate got up, walked to the front, and handed England his blank paper. I would not have been surprised later to learn that he had walked downtown and cast himself off the 5th Street Bridge into the dark arms of the Brazos River. Pudgy scribbled away as though he were George Frideric Handel incomprehensibly composing *The Messiah* in twenty-four incomprehensible days.

Ted L. Estess

My friend Judith McCleary, who later turned hippie and married an alcoholic, and I walked out of the room together. We would both receive a B, mine with the alleged help of some sawing and hammering. Both of us were defeated, and we knew it.

But exiting into the light of May, we burst into a duet of harmonious laughter. It was a laughter of release and recognition. In a Greek drama, the moment would be called an *anagnorisis*, a recognition, a moment when we see into ourselves and our situations. Judith and I did not have to have perfect pitch. We were incapable of acquiring perfect pitch. In the exam, a musical genius had exposed our ineptitude—our incapacity, our not-being-able-to—and, because of that, we could walk out into the fresh air of a late spring day and enjoy ourselves all the more.

It occurs to me today that in the midst of our laughter that I might have taken Judith's hand and walked together with her toward the statue of Judge Baylor across from the music school and said, "Lovely Judith, you and I have learned something quite by accident at the end of our first collegiate year. We have learned that we can be free from the curse of every musician, which is the gnawing to be perfect. Nicholas England tried to teach us to be bi-dexterous in our rhythms, but he failed, as did we. Lovely Judith, let's skip all the way to the statue, and right there before the Judge, let's dance the night away."

It has taken me a long time to recognize what I learned that May afternoon. Some days, I forget it still. I didn't learn something true *about* living a life. Rather, something true happened to me. For the first time I experienced the difference between truth-as-knowledge-about and truth-as-happening. That afternoon, it happened. For a moment, I was released from the fear of making mistakes, from the craving to be perfect. For a while, being imperfect—being incapable—even seemed a good thing to be. I also glimpsed the fact that a person can have perfect pitch, make straight A's, and still flunk life.

What I didn't know that afternoon was that come autumn, lovely Judith and I would be worried English majors. By then, we would have forgotten what we had learned by way of failure barely three months earlier. That's the way it is with things we really need to learn in life: we learn them, if only for a season; then we forget them; then we have to learn them again, again, and again.

Fishing Spirit Lake

My learning took another turn in the semester when I began reading W. H. Auden, T. S. Eliot, Dylan Thomas, and other poets of their ilk. I tried Wallace Stevens, but was not ready for him. I walked across campus with Eliot's words reverberating with my own mounting sense of irony, uncertainty, and doubt:

> In a minute there is time
> For decisions and revisions which a minute will reverse.
>
> That is not what I meant at all.
> That is not it, at all. . . .

But remembering my growing up days in rural Mississippi, I luxuriated with Dylan Thomas' boisterous lines:

> Now as I was young and easy under the apple boughs
> About the lilting house and happy as the grass was green,
> The night above the dingle starry,
> Time let me hail and climb
> Golden in the heydays of his eyes. . . .

Looking back, I suppose that if I could hold such incongruous lines from such disparate poets as Eliot and Thomas together, maybe Nicholas England had not completely failed: maybe I could get counter-rhythms of sensibility going within myself.

One night I went to bed in 312 Martin Hall intending, as I often did, to get up early to study for Professor Clement Goode's British Lit class. At the time we were reading the great Romantics, Wordsworth, Shelley, Keats, and Byron. It was from Goode's mouth that I first heard the words "negative capability." He talked as if this were a good thing. After all, Goode told us, Keats thought that Shakespeare, more than any other writer, manifests this capacity. By that time, I had learned what the word "oxymoron" means. It occurred to me that Keats' negative capability was a perfect example of an oxymoron. After all, how could a negative be a "capability?" Was Keats suggesting that an incapacity is a positive acquisition, even a worthy, perhaps a necessary achievement? To that point, I had been aiming to develop positive capabilities, such as the capacity to write and think, to play the piano, to make and refute arguments. I was puzzled—maybe, for the first time in my life, thoroughly puzzled—by Keats' suggesting and Goode's recommending a different capacity of being, specifically, the capacity "of being in uncertainties, Mysteries, doubts...."

That particular night in Martin Hall, as was my custom, I set the timer on my Magnavox Hi-Fi so as to wake up early to finish preparation for Professor's Goode's exam. That Magnavox was the first major purchase I made in my life. It was May of 1958. I was a junior in high school, and my parents went with me to the Brown Music Store on Capitol Street in Jackson, Mississippi. I paid $212 of my own money, tax included, for my Hi-Fi.

My father couldn't believe it. Why would a young man want to pay that kind of money so he could listen to Beethoven and Mozart? I now appreciate that my father tolerated what he did not understand. It's a good quality for a parent to have. One morning at breakfast I asked him if he thought I should order the complete set of Arthur Rubenstein's playing the five Beethoven piano concertos from the RCA record club. I actually wanted him to confirm me in my inclination to do just that. Instead, he asked, "Well, do you need all five?"

My father did not comprehend that listening to Arthur Rubenstein play Beethoven has nothing to do with need, at least in the ordinary sense of the word. It has to do with enjoyment and the desire to adorn life. I didn't have a way of understanding—if that is possible—such a need until I studied *King Lear* with Professor Goode in that British Lit class. I read about Lear's being stripped by his two devilish daughters of all the accoutrements of royalty. Pressing him to explain why he "needs" the remnants of a retinue and other symbols of his former regal state, the anguished old king says to his daughters, "Reason not the need," which is to say that, in proportion, things that adorn life are self-justifying. But confronted with what I took to be a slight rebuke in my father's question, I ordered only the *Emperor*. I have never gotten around to the other four.

The *Emperor* was poised to wake me that morning. When the timer clicked, I dropped quickly down out of the top bunk so as not to wake my roommate, who was an earthy preacher-boy from Aztec, New Mexico, named Jerry Wayne Brown. I stopped the record and started my exercise. I had lately read the Canadian Air Force book on getting a workout in twelve minutes, and it seemed a good thing for a good young man to do. I was up to the twentieth push-up when Brown turned over and asked, "What the hell are you doing, Estess? It's two o'clock in the morning."

Another time, I walked into 312 Martin after midnight and I found Brown dead out asleep on his knees with his head resting on his bed. "What the hell are you doing, Brown?" I asked. There he had been, on his knees, having fallen asleep doing what his momma had taught him to do every night.

Now and again, it occurred to Brown and me that not all our classmates were exercising their positive capabilities. One day Brown crashed into the room outraged that a linebacker had bragged at the training table that he had *done it* with one of the cleaning women, right on his bed in Martin Hall. He said he gave her five dollars. I never was clear about the source of Brown's outrage, whether he thought the woman had been misused, or whether he felt the linebacker had paid too much, or whether he regretted not doing the same. I don't remember the linebacker's name, but I do know he turned Republican, got elected to high office, was named an outstanding Baylor graduate, and died young.

Pleasure, however much we wanted it, was not our calling. It reminds me of a story that Grady Nutt told about Wayland Baptist College. Nutt was a Baylor graduate who was a preacher before he turned full-time humorist and made the big-time as a regular on a TV-show called *Hee-Haw*. The last news I had of him was from WWL radio out of New Orleans, Louisiana. I was visiting Mississippi, when WWL reported one morning that Grady Nutt had been killed in a plane crash, flying from Cullman, Alabama, to Louisville, Kentucky. The pilot had cautioned about bad weather, but Nutt had insisted that he had to get home to his wife and kids.

Before making the mistake of wanting to get home too bad, Nutt once told me that you could get kicked out of Wayland Baptist College for one of four things: smokin', drinkin', dancin', or wantin' to. Nutt said they caught him wantin' to.

At Baylor I spent a good deal of time wantin' to. Besides wantin' to, I see now that I longed after two things. I wanted to be—I'm embarrassed to say it—I wanted to be holy or great. Fortunately, I failed at both.

I of course could not in those years know that a few years later I would marry a classmate named Sybil Pittman and that we would explore the regions beneath the clothing without getting into any trouble and that we, some years later, would have a son named Barrett. Nor could I know that when Barrett was twelve years old, the three of us would find ourselves one summer in the desert of New Mexico and that I would, for reasons unknown, find myself trying to explain to him about my early compulsion to be either great or holy, preferably both.

Straightaway, Barrett understood wanting to be great; he, after all, played baseball. You will never meet a baseball player who sets out to be ordinary. Average ain't good enough.

In his twelfth summer, Barrett found the desire for holiness completely incomprehensible. I told him that at times when I was in college that I could imagine myself becoming a monk, if Baptists had monks. After I explained what a monk is, he was dumbfounded all the more.

The subject of monks came up because, at Sybil's insistence, we were going to vesper services at a monastery called Christ of the Desert. Neither Barrett nor I were very much interested in vesper services. We weren't even sure what vesper services were, but that didn't deter Sybil. At about 4 p.m. that day we drove off the highway, crossed over a cattle gap, and headed across what turned out to be twelve miles of bad desert road. Sybil didn't have precise directions. "It's not far," she insisted.

Later, when driving out, we would be frightened. It had rained and the red dirt road was slippery. Several times the car's tires spun and we couldn't get up a hill. One time we slid backwards and I couldn't control the wheels. We laid sagebrush on the road to improve our traction. Sybil's response bordered on garden-variety hysteria. She ordered Barrett out of the car to walk, saying to me, "You can fall off the road if you want to, but I'm not going to let you kill Barrett and me." I muttered something about her getting us into the mess in the first place. The two of them walked alongside the car as I again slid to the edge. Sybil announced that we would spend the night in the car, right there on the slippery desert road. Barrett said we could make it out and we did.

But driving in, Sybil had wanted us to experience vespers at that monastery down the road from Ghost Ranch where Georgia O'Keeffe had her summer house. I told Barrett about Georgia O'Keeffe and about how she had escaped to the desert and about one of my favorite paintings of hers. In a painting of the night at Ghost Ranch, Georgia O'Keeffe has a ladder going up from the desert floor. It looks as though one can step right up from the ladder onto the moon.

Sybil had turned spiritual by that time in life, which is what prompted our journey to Christ of the Desert in the first place. She wanted to taste, even for an hour or two, the godly life. She wanted to step up out of the desert and onto the moon. Spiritualism is a great temptation to women, Episcopalians, and poets. Sybil was all three.

"Yes," I said to Barrett as we drove in, "I can understand why these men spend their lives in the desert." Hearkening back to my undergraduate years, I talked to him about the monastic ideal and the rule of Saint Benedict and medieval monasteries, and about the desire to commit oneself to meditation and prayer for the purification of one's soul and the glory of God. I told him that for monks the end of man is to glorify God and to enjoy Him forever. He didn't understand the word "end." I explained that it means one's purpose in life, the ultimate thing that directs and gives meaning to everything one does. He asked if everybody has to have one, and I told him that it helps. I told him that it's what gets the monks together seven times a day to pray, beginning at four in the morning. Then they work in the garden and look after pilgrims who come to the desert in retreat from what they take to be the desert of life in the ordinary world.

As the eleven monks and we ten pilgrims filed out of the abbey, our clothes reeked with the sweet smell of incense that had carried the purified prayers aloft. At that moment my old inclination returned. I thought, then and there, of walking out with those monks, leaving Sybil and Barrett to wonder whether or not I had lost my mind. Instead, I thought, *That's* what I'll do. I'll get a few friends and maybe some students and we'll drive out here and spend a week on retreat. We'll taste holy solitude in the desert.

"Yes," I told Barrett, "in the twelfth century I would have been a monk." What I didn't fully explain to him was that, in many ways, I had in my youth made a good try at being the Baptist-equivalent. He wasn't impressed. He said that the incense stank and the monks prayed too long. He figured that they didn't play baseball either. He wanted to know why one of the monks looked angry and another seemed bored. He added that if you have to live in the desert to have an end in life, he didn't want one.

Looking back at my teen and college years, I see that I inclined toward purity much of the time. I spent the best part of my youth bartering milquetoast goodness for approval. The motivation was as much fear of rejection as high spiritual purpose. I never sinned enough to feel really good and saved. But part of me wanted to do what those few monks do out there in the desert near Ghost Ranch: make it all pure and holy.

Had a monk walked out of the desert onto the campus of Baylor University on a Tuesday afternoon in the summer of 1964 and had stopped me at the corner of 5th and Speight and said, "Come live in the desert with us for a year or two," I may well have signed up right on the spot. Friends of mine joined the Peace Corps. I might have taken to the desert. With one bold stroke, I would have solved a lot of problems.

That's likely the reason why my friend Jerry Welch made an unexpected announcement to me one night in that summer. Welch turned out to be a psychotherapist in South Carolina, but in July of 1964 he was an ironic, depressive philosophy major who knew more about Albert Camus than he did about living an ordinary day. Welch and I talked about the weightiness of existence and Bergman movies, and despaired of meaning in life and wondered if belief in God were philosophical suicide. We were the life of any party, not that we went to any.

Welch had bought two six-packs of Miller High Life with which to celebrate his twenty-second birthday. We were at the room that he and I shared down 8th Street below the Browning Library on the Baylor campus. All was not right with the world. But there we were, I with T. S. Eliot, revising and reversing, while Welch swilled the High Life. I would not yet drink the stuff. My brother Roy always said that beer looks like horse piss. That was enough to deter me.

Welch was into the second six-pack when he came over to the bed where I languished on sheets grown damp from the swamp fan. I muttered some self-indulging lament. Welch, with a Miller in one hand and a Winston in the other, leaned over the side of the bed and turned his eagle beak and scabrous face down at me. Out of the shadows I heard a deep boom: "Estess. You're not *God*."

It is unlikely that many people in East Waco or elsewhere were waiting for such an announcement to emanate from a damp room inhabited by a couple of ironic-depressive Baylor seniors during the great heat wave of 1964, but the news did get my attention. I am unsure why Welch without provocation from me—other than that I wasn't into the High Life—pronounced this judgment. Perhaps it was because I was monomaniacal about reading books and being a good boy.

His words dug deep. It hadn't occurred to me by that time that one good reason to have a God—even a half dozen gods—is that having a god relieves you of the necessity of being one. If you are not god, you can relax and enjoy yourself, have a good time, even be a lowdown scoundrel if you want to.

I didn't know exactly what to make of Welch's proclamation. I was left to wonder whether Welch was engaging in an alcoholic spasm of feckless speculation or whether he was saying something that, could I embrace it, might have consequences for the living of a satisfying, if unremarkable, life. Perhaps he was voicing a truth that needed to happen to me.

In time, I saw that Welch had indeed said something I needed to hear. Now, I am fully prepared to acknowledge that normal people are not like me. For them, Welch's *kergyma*, his message, may not be a big deal. For me, it's an insight that one can miss. It's so basic that we are given to ignore or forget it. *You're not God.*

All kinds of things followed. For instance, I gave up the desire to be pure or great. I wasn't up to it. I realized that I couldn't name a single pure great man who was worth a shit as a husband and father. Greatness and family don't mix. Purity neither, which is to say that if you are deciding on a husband or a wife, don't look for a god or goddess. Saints are bad risks, too. Take after someone who is capable of living an ordinary, finite, all too human life, full of uncertainties, mysteries, failures, mistakes, and wonders.

## A Ball in a Box

For a good deal of my life, I was reluctant to have fun. My parents and the Baptists conspired to make me suspicious of it. My parents did so by emphasizing the importance of work in this world, the Baptists by emphasizing preparation for living in the other world. Early on, they both made it plain that whatever I was put on this earth to do, it wasn't to enjoy myself.

The only thing that really counted for Baptists was getting me saved. So I spent the better part of my youth wondering if I were. Other guys were playing ball and chasing girls, and here I was worrying about being saved. I must have concluded that it is inadvisable to have fun unless you are, and I could never be sure.

It reminds me of Miss Kitty Boo Barefoot who was Sybil's Sunday School teacher in the Baptist Church in Poplarville, Mississippi. Miss Kitty Boo also doubled as the math teacher and librarian in the high school. But that was subsidiary to her principal mission, the religious and moral instruction of fifteen vigorously pubescent Baptist girls on Sunday mornings.

Miss Kitty Boo was renowned for the size of her bosom. It was said that she had not seen her navel in twenty years. It was also said that the high school physics teacher, a bright young man named Grubbs, had devised a mathematical formula with which to calculate the load-bearing requirements of the human skeleton sufficient to tote Miss Kitty Boo's mammary system.

Now this dedicated teacher of youth became distraught when she heard that some young people in town were said to be dancing. So one Sunday morning Miss Kitty Boo brought the concern to her Baptists girls, some of whom, she feared, might be about to embark on the mission of having fun. She looked around the room, suspecting that Jo Ann and certainly Carla—both of whose ample young bosoms had themselves attracted the attention of the high school physics teacher—had been dancing the night before, and maybe worse.

"Girls," Miss Kitty Boo said, her bosom heaving in waves, "I been prayin' about it, and the Lord has laid it right here, right here on my heart." With that, Miss Kitty Boo smacked her right hand down into the middle of her left breast. For a few seconds, the hand disappeared. "Some of your mommas and daddies might tell you different," she said, "but this is something I jest got to get off my chest. I said to myself, 'Kitty Boo, what if something happens to you before you get a chance to tell your girls?' So this morning I want you girls to know: the Lord told me, 'Kitty Boo, you ought-un to dance.' And I'm *not* gonna do it."

It seems that this revelation from the Lord came as good news to Miss Kitty Boo's husband, who was named Christopher Columbus Barefoot. At the post office the next morning, Mister Chris said to Charlie Pitts: "Yep, Charlie, I'm damn sho' glad the Lord told Kitty Boo not to take me dancin'. I mighta drownt in her tits."

Charlie Pitts thought that was so funny he told it all over town. Charlie asked everybody he saw, "You know whut Christopher Columbus told me at the post office the other morning? He told me that he sho' wuz glad that the Lord told Kitty Boo not to take him dancin'. Said he mighta drownt in her tits."

When we were young and Baptist at Baylor and sharing that musty room in the summer of 1964, Jerry Welch and I avoided dancing and other fun things. Welch's deep, sardonic laughter echoed through the room day and night. By that time, irony and sarcasm had pretty well eroded everything we had ever tried to believe. We were stuck in irony, which is to be suspended in the middle, unattached, uncommitted, and alone. Irony, Kierkegaard said, can negate the very grounds of one's existence.

It reminds me of something Bill Martin once said. Bill is an old Baptist who taught for decades at Rice University and who made a hit with his biography of Billy Graham. Bill once thought he had lost his father to a serious illness, but he got him back. Bill was giving a religious reading of the event when he said, "People sometimes ask me what I believe. I tell them I believe as much as I can."

That summer in Waco, Jerry Welch and I aimed to believe as little as we could. We took uncritical believing to be something on the order of farting at the dinner table. It adds aroma to an occasion but one wants it to disperse as soon as possible. Welch and I systematically sought not to believe or to disbelieve. It seemed better that way. At least we would not be caught making a mistake.

It brings to mind the trip Welch and I made to Miami for the wedding of two of our Baylor friends. We were slightly amazed that anybody we knew would be able to promise anything until death do us part. We got shaky when we promised to meet somebody for lunch on Monday.

Heading out of Waco on a Thursday afternoon, Welch's white 1958 Dodge was running good, its wide fins splitting the air. All afternoon and through the night, we sped across Louisiana bayous, along the Mississippi coast, and on east and south into Florida. Going about eighty-five just beyond Tallahassee, we passed two guys on Harley Davidsons at dawn. As we passed, Welch shot them the bird. In the purplish light of sunrise, the horizon had the color of a bad bruise.

On down the boot of Florida we sped, laughing, or sneering, at everything and everyone we saw, thirteen hundred miles in less than twenty-four hours. "Look at that bastard," Welch shouted. "Get outta the road, you asshole. You trying to kill somebody?" His laugh resounded through the hot air as we trailed irony and sarcasm the length of the Sunshine State.

Once there we changed clothes and went to the rehearsal and then to the party at the bride's house, where at one point several of us gathered around her daffy aunt. The aunt was a weasely little woman. Her shiny green eyes glistened in the bright light of the room. Talking to her, I thought she must be standing in a hole, so short she was. Her face looked like it was made from lizard skin. Too much time in the Sunshine State does that to you: it gives you a lizard face.

This little woman was a sunny believer. There wasn't anything she didn't believe, but I couldn't detect any defining core or denominational stamp: she believed it all, spiritualisms East and West, mystical transformations of a fervent sort, Jesus and Buddha with psychological integration and Christian Science stirred in—she had some of it all. She was a Jungian in lizard skin, with bliss that would have made Joseph Campbell proud.

We stood around her—Welch and I and another Baylor friend

named Harrison Kohler—listening to this weasely woman with a lizard face drone on about her beliefs. With her spiritual eyes glistening in the light of the chandelier that hung overhead, she was admiring a flower on the dining room table. I looked across that flower to see Welch, smirking at her side. Standing beside him, Kohler nodded and feigned interest.

"Just look at this beautiful flower," she exclaimed. We three young Baptists stared at the Bird of Paradise, that peacock of flowers. The flower had the color of the bruised dawn of that day, bluish purple, burnt orange, and red. "How could anyone look at this Bird of Paradise," she asked, "and not believe in God?"

Her question puts in mind something that one of Walker Percy's characters says. He says he is disgusted with two kinds of assholes: believers and non-believers. This woman was a believing asshole.

Back then, whenever Welch and I encountered believing assholes, we hooted at the fragility of their thinking. When we happened upon unbelieving assholes, we lamented their shallowness and laughed at the incoherency of their thought. Most of them, we contended, had no more idea of why they got up in the morning than a goose. We had it both ways; we played both sides of the street. We were determined to be neither believing assholes nor unbelieving assholes. We were suspended in the ironical middle. You could call us borderline assholes.

"How," this fervent believer asked, "how could anyone look at this beautiful flower and not believe in God?"

None of us knew what to say. Kohler, who would do nothing to offend, dropped his eyes. Though not as given to irony as Welch and I, Kohler wasn't going to commit himself. Neither was he going to be impolite. If his momma and daddy had taught Kohler anything, they had taught him to be a nice boy. Welch took a drag on his Winston and looked at me. His grayish eyes were sunk into an ashen face. Our eyes met, impassive and distant. Silence abounded.

Squinting through Winston smoke, our friend's aunt waited for a reply, her now teary eyes upturned at Welch. I expected to see Welch slowly shift the Winston to his left hand and with the right reach down past that fervent woman's lizardy face and seize that Bird of Paradise by the throat. I expected him to squeeze his hand around the lovely bird and crush paradise between his nicotine-stained fingers. Then, as though enacting her worst nightmare, he would lean down to that glimmering face and in his deepest, most sardonic tone, announce, "That's what I think of *that*."

Instead, Welch pursed his lips and took a drag on his Winston as I mumbled, "Yes, ma'am, that sure is a beautiful flower." Welch emitted a soft, ironic chuckle. Kohler smiled and nodded. All of us shuffled awkwardly around that little woman with her very own proof for the existence of God, a bluish purple, burnt orange and red Bird of Paradise.

After midnight the next night, Welch and I were driving up the Sunshine State Parkway when a state trooper pulled us over. "You fellows in a hurry?" he asked. From the back seat where I was lying down, I heard Welch's deep voice: "Yes sir . . . . No sir . . . . Yes sir . . . . No sir." To hear Welch kowtow to that officer of the law, one would have thought that he was president of the Tallahassee Jaycees. Where was the irony now? "Estess, how much money you got?" he asked of me. Taking out my final ten bucks, I passed it over the seat to Welch. He handed the trooper twenty-five dollars and we headed off, still driving eighty-five.

"You know what I wanted to do when she shoved that Bird of Paradise in my face?" Welch asked me as we drove on. "I wanted to reach right over and crush that goddamn flower in my hand. That's what I wanted to do." Our sardonic laughs reverberated from Tallahassee all the way to Apalachicola.

Jerry Welch and I were something like that picture of Jean-Paul Sartre that appeared about that time on the cover of *Life* magazine. Sartre had made himself famous writing books with titles like *Nausea* and *No Exit* and *Being and Nothingness*. On the cover of *Life*, Jean-Paul was pictured standing alone on an iceberg, floating in the middle of the North Sea.

That's what Welch and I were, two isolates floating on an iceberg in the middle of a frigid sea.

Toward the end of that summer, I went to the Trailways bus station in Waco on a hot Sunday afternoon. The heat rose in waves from the street, giving the air an oily sheen. I had arrived in Texas at that bus station four years earlier, carrying all my stuff in two suitcases.

Four years later and I was burnt out on winning friends and influencing people. That afternoon I enacted that burned-out feeling by bidding farewell to the Baylor coed who had been my sometimes sweetheart for a couple of years. She was a smart and savvy girl from the Mississippi Delta who had no business being entangled with the likes of me. In saying goodbye, I gave her a gift, something that I had bought for her months earlier. Looking at her through the green glass, I saw her wipe tears from her eyes. I wondered why the hell I waited until I said goodbye to give her that gift. Maybe it was a guilt offering. I haven't seen or heard from her since and suppose I never will.

What I didn't see at the station that day was that the gift I presented to my Delta sweetheart was an image of myself. It was a pendant made of delicate silver filigree. There was an outer box with an inner ball. A ball in a box. The ball rolled free, unattached, confined, tightly so.

When I finished college, I was rolling around in a box largely of my own making. My Mississippi and Baptist life had been ripped up by the roots, which now dangled limp in the hot Texas air. At the time I would have thought it shameful to tell my skeptical friends about my previous life in Mississippi, such as the times when I went possum hunting on cold winter nights or when I went with friends on a Sunday night after church and liberated watermelons from a farmer's patch or when I floated down Magee's Creek with buddies in July and camped on the sandbar and swam together on a June afternoon. In the summer of 1964 a Mississippian was not a good thing to be.

Neither did I like telling people I was going to the Southern Baptist Seminary. Whenever someone asked me what I was going to do in the fall, I would slur the words and say, "I'm goin' to study theology at Suthern-Semnar-in-LousvilKentucky." People probably thought I had a speech impediment, slurring my words like that. I didn't recognize it at the time, but my speech was impaired: I couldn't speak for myself.

By the end of my collegiate years, I had lost my voice. I had arrived in Waco blithely mouthing things I had taken in from Baptists and other folks in Mississippi. After four years of books, I was pretty much a mute rolling around in a box. If becoming aware of my incapacities was a good thing, I was on the way; but I was still a long way from Keats' "negative capability," which is, you remember, the capacity "of being in uncertainties, Mysteries, doubts without any irritable reaching after fact and reason. . . ."

Fishing Spirit Lake

My box was constructed of ideas, concepts and abstractions, and arguments of infinite variety. I could entertain any position but held none, at least not on consecutive days. I could analyze any argument but was grounded by few. I bathed in Beethoven and Chopin and daydreamed a lot. I was a romantic, always putting just beyond my grasp the thing I really wanted. Infinitely to defer gratification, that was my way to be.

One encouraging thing was that some friends were in a similar box and were also heading off to Louisville that fall. None of us likely would have gone alone. Our boxes, as it were, were sitting on the same iceberg in the same frigid sea.

So we floated north on our iceberg, up from the Brazos in the deep heart of Texas to the borderlands of Kentucky on the banks of the Ohio, to what folks called the land of beautiful horses and fast women. While it would never be that for us, we hoped to find in Kentucky what we hadn't found in Texas: a life for ourselves. Little did we know that in Kentucky, our teachers would come at us with crowbars and ice axes.

## Bounded Grace

## I

Arriving in Kentucky, my buddies gave scant attention to rainbows or moonlight, rain or snow or anything from above—or from below, for that matter. Our eyes, by and large, were turned inward. I went so far as to give up baseball. I didn't follow the pennant races or the World Series and didn't go when several guys from the dormitory drove up to Cincinnati to see Sandy Koufax pitch against the Reds. I told them I had to finish my paper on Karl Barth's doctrine of justification for Professor Mueller. In my four years in Louisville, Kentucky, I made it to Churchill Downs two times and drank one mint julep.

A night on the town for my friends and me was to head to the art theater on Bardstown Road to catch another Bergman movie. We especially liked films in which some poor soul suffered the death of God. In one, an ashened guy all dressed in black and a beautiful young woman dressed in white rowed a small boat out to a windswept island for a holiday. She spent the best part of the movie screaming and in tears. He stared into the distance a lot and seemed unhappy. We liked it a lot.

Soon after we arrived in Louisville, six of us seminarians took out for 4th Street on a Saturday night. Other young men walked that lively street with us that night, also out for a break from the routine of their week. Those young soldiers from Fort Knox turned into a bar not far from the river, aiming to pick up a girl if they could. Failing that, they would catch a movie or go for a ride on the Delta Queen, then have a few more beers.

Following my lead, my group turned into a side alley and went up some dimly lit stairs above the Tom McAnn shoe store on 4th Street where Actors Theater of Louisville was struggling to get started. We sat down in folding chairs and waited for the show, a double-bill of Edward Albee's *The Zoo Story* and *American Dream*.

Ted L. Estess

Decades later, Albee was a faculty colleague of mine in Houston. One evening I told him about my encountering his work on 4th Street in Louisville, Kentucky, above a Tom McAnn shoe store. He liked the part about the shoe store. I think he thinks that people appreciate his plays more if the theater is hard to find and the seats are uncomfortable. He's probably right.

Afterwards, we walked down 4th Street, pleased with ourselves for having spent a serious, worthwhile night, worthwhile because it was serious. We talked about Albee and the inanity of the American dream.

In those days our lives were charged with a heightened sense of importance. It is not that we were egoistic: if anything, we probably lacked what psychotherapists might call sufficient ego structure. But among us seminarians, narcissistic seriousness reached epidemic proportions. We lived in a twenty-four-hour-a-day, seven-day-a-week T-Group. "Getting to Know Me"—I mean "You"—was our theme song, but we couldn't sing the melody.

There was little to temper the seriousness. In fact, we thought ourselves lucky to be accepted into a program in the psychiatric ward of Norton Hospital led by Professor Samuel Southard. Studying the eclipse of God at the seminary was not enough; we had to study the tortured depths of other troubled psyches in our spare time.

It was also thought that working in a psychiatric ward would be good preparation for prospective ministers, not that all of us aspired to that noble calling. I didn't: I already knew that I wanted to head to a Ph.D. program and a university job. But it was thought that young ministers would be better equipped to work with the typical congregation on the theory that churches are a good deal like psychiatric hospitals. I suppose the same goes for universities.

The first night on the ward, four of us seminarians-in-training-to-work-as-nursing-aides gathered with Sego, who was the head psychiatric nurse on the night shift. We were dressed in hospital white as though we were there to peddle ice cream. Sego bit the tip of his cigarette, slightly baring his teeth as he did. He took short, rapid puffs, and moved his hand in rhythm with his swinging foot, all the time pushing smoke through his clenched teeth. His glee was irrepressible. He was a sadistic sonnafabitch.

"You're Estess?" he asked. "You go down to Room 21. Mary's there.

She's eighteen-years old. Catatonic stupor. Won't eat, won't talk. She says there's glass in her food. Her father's a bastard, her mother's a bitch. See what you can do with her in thirty minutes." Sego chuckled and took three quick puffs and blew the smoke through his teeth, all the time stirring the air with his foot.

As I turned off the well-lighted hallway, I thought at first that the room was empty; but as my eyes accustomed to the shadows, I saw the back of this frail figure standing immobile on the opposite side of the bed, staring into the corner. "Hello, Mary," I said, "my name is Ted. I've come to sit with you. I'm only going to stay thirty minutes. I'll just be here waiting, okay, Mary? Mary?" I sat and waited, now and again mumbling a few words when the oppressive silence became too much to bear. Mary stood less than ten feet away, but I had never felt more alone. For the last ten minutes, I went over and stood by her. She didn't turn her face toward me. What few words I could think to speak fell from my lips like bits of confetti drifting down into a dark well. "I'll come back to see you again, okay, Mary?" I left her as I found her, standing, immobile, on the opposite side of the bed, staring into the corner.

The following Saturday morning I was the nursing aide assigned to roll Mary to the room where she was to receive electro-convulsive therapy. In the treatment room, I assisted in attaching the leather straps to her arms and legs. I stood at her feet as the doctor and nurse inserted the mouth guard, secured her head in a leather bonnet, attached the electrical apparatus, and turned the switch. Mary's frail body convulsed on the table, every limb straining against the straps. Tinges of white foam slipped from the corners of her mouth. Her head jerked to break free. When I visited her in her room one evening the following week, she was staring into the corner, still mute.

The next week our group of interns sat in a hospital conference room. Professor Southard was there to look us over and offer his assessment of how we were doing.

"Welch here"—Southard said with a smirky smile showing on his smirky face—"now Welch is like one of those mortars we used in the army. He stays outside the circle and occasionally tosses in a shell. It explodes and takes attention away from him. Then he circles around to change positions. Then he tosses in another shell, but he stays outside the circle."

Southard paused, looked around the group, and said, "We're not going to let him get away with that, are we, men?"

I'm glad he's not saying that about me, I thought, as Southard turned to Kohler. "Now, Kohler there is a tortoise. He moves along, steady and dependable, but he stays in his shell most of the time. Not much is getting through, not much is coming out." Southard stared at Kohler, all the time keeping that crooked smile in place.

Harrison chuckled an embarrassed chuckle. With a broad Grand Prairie, Texas, grin on his soft face, he said, "I guess so, Dr. Southard."

"I know so," Southard replied. With his slick black hair and his dark brown suit and dark, Bogart-eyes, Southard seemed as though he had stepped out of a film noir to pronounce an ultimatum. "But Kohler," he said, "is a nice tortoise. You are a nice tortoise, aren't you, Kohler?"

We all knowingly chuckled, thinking he had Harry about right. A few of us tried ourselves to put on a smirky smile.

"McArthur here," Southard said, "he still thinks he can make it like he did in the frat house down at Vanderbilt." We Texans had met Frank McArthur the first week in Louisville and had quickly accepted him into our group, if for no other reason than that he was altogether different from us. A native of New Orleans, McArthur had no qualms about having a good time. Members of my group had spent our four collegiate years reading philosophy, literature, and theology. Frank, who was short and rotund in the way of Lou Costello, spent his years having a good time and making everybody around him laugh. Before having the misfortune to meet up with us, he had drunk a good bit of Bourbon but had never seen a Bergman movie.

Southard continued. "McArthur will learn. All of you men will learn: this world is not a frat house. These patients are not fraternity brothers. You won't be able to make them laugh, much less make them happy. They will not make you happy. If you want to help them, you've got to get out of the frat house and into the hospital. Do you understand, McArthur?"

McArthur took a nervous drag on his Lucky Strike and said, "Yes sir, Dr. Southard, yes sir. I understand, Dr. Southard, yes sir, I understand." From the perimeter we heard Welch's laughter tossed into the circle like a mortar shell. McArthur no doubt was wondering why the hell he had allowed Welch to persuade him to enter the program with Southard in the first place.

"Dr. Southard," Welch said, "what about Estess? You forgot about Estess."

"Oh Estess, yes, Estess," our teacher said, "Estess is easy to forget. He doesn't say much, does he? Rabbit Estess is the hiding man. He's hiding in the bushes. We'll wait until he's ready to come out, won't we?"

Southard turned and looked at me with as stern and knowing a look as I've ever encountered. He smiled, this time without a smirk. He said, "We'll wait."

For a long time in the silence of that room, Southard and my friends smiled and looked at me. I thought again of Mary of the catatonic stupor, the one who had lost her voice, who had yet to find words for her self, the one whom the doctor could not shake into speech. In the meantime—and it was a *mean* time—they kept on smiling and waiting.

"You can do without many things," Elie Wiesel likes to say, "but you cannot do without a teacher."

My friends and I seemed somehow to know that when we were in Louisville, for we gravitated to the good teachers. Southard was the chief of the lot, though at the time I did not altogether understand what he was doing. I did know that he had an uncanny way of making each of us anxious and uncertain about ourselves.

I think now that I know what he was up to. I think he was aiming always to break down our sense of self-sufficiency. I've never known a man less impressed by what other men and women did or less interested in what they thought of him than Sam Southard. Nothing human seemed to impress or surprise him. He was not afraid of anything either. Southard exuded this air, however, not because he thought he was sufficient unto himself. The source of his way of being in the world was something altogether different. I'll try to explain.

Southard knew that we were successful young men, but he also believed that whatever success we might achieve would be forever insufficient to satisfy. We would always wonder whether we had done enough. We would always need one more round of applause.

Southard, therefore, sought to break down, cruelly if need be, our tendency to rely on our positive capacities, on what we did—or accomplished or acquired—to secure our well-being. In doing so, he sought to provoke us into relationship with one another. We had to depend on each other to make it through those weeks in the psychiatric hospital and in the group and individual therapy sessions that followed. What we did, we were to do in relationship.

He then counted on our coming to see that the approval of friends, as rich and consoling as that might be, would itself be insufficient. "Your friends will not be enough," he said one day. "They will let you down. Remember Peter in the Garden."

Paradoxically, then, in order to learn the fragility of friendship, we had first to learn to rely on friends; and, if we did, Southard thought, we would discover what he wanted us to discover: that, unlike what nearly every late adolescent is given to think, friendship alone, as crucial and indispensable as it is, is insufficient as a foundation for life. One can never do enough and never get enough approval from others to satisfy, or so it now seems to me that Southard thought. Our puny individual egos are forever screaming for love and approval.

So what was the point for him? The point was to exhaust human resources and thereby intensify desperation to the point that we would depend on grace, as Martin Luther would say, on *sola gratia*, on the grace that the Baptists always call *amazing*. We would recognize our own insufficiency and laugh at it and come to see that we were clowns ever to think that we could be sufficient unto ourselves. We would, in turn, recognize the fallibility of friends and the limitations of their approval, and enjoy them all the more for it. When they disappointed us, as surely they would, we would tell them that they had done so, have a good laugh, and forget it. They would do the same with us. In short, Southard was teaching me not only that I am not God but also that neither is anyone else.

Southard was a Calvinist, one of few remaining in captivity. Calvinists, I sometimes think, need to be protected under the Endangered Species Act. Southard thus wanted us to do with each other what he thought his Calvinist God does with all human creatures, judge, forgive, enjoy, and have a good laugh. The Calvinist God is to human beings as a dramatist is to the players on a stage: having already written the script that is being played out, he is an interested observer. He can sit back and watch the play. That was precisely the relationship that Southard had with his students: knowing that the outcome did not ultimately depend on anything that he was or on anything that he did, he simply watched and enjoyed the play as it unfolded.

Southard also thought that if we could come to depend on grace beyond ourselves, Welch would stop throwing mortar shells from the perimeter and would come into the circle of friends; Kohler would come out of his shell and let others get to him; McArthur would stop trying to make people like him as though that would make him happy; and Rabbit Estess would step from behind the bushes and stand forth and say something without being afraid of making a mistake, not in his own strength but in *sola gratia*.

Several decades hence, I'm not sure, but I think that this was what Southard was trying to teach. The next time I see Welch and Kohler and McArthur—we still get together every year or so—I'm going to ask them, "Is this what Southard had in mind?"

If Welch and I could transport ourselves back to our rooms in the seminary, I can very well imagine his taking a slow drag on his Winston, and in his deep, sardonic voice, saying, "That's a good question, Estess. That's a damn good question. Why don't you try to answer it sometimes."

# II

What about it? Grace, I mean. For one thing, grace seems to be one of those old words that we can hardly do without, which reminds me of something that Clov shouts to Hamm in Samuel Beckett's *Endgame*. In response to Hamm's complaint about something that he has said, Clov screams, "I use the words you taught me. If they don't mean anything any more, teach me others. Or let me be silent." Over the years, I've come to think that grace is one of those words that we have to use until a better one comes along.

For myself, I've always been reluctant to depend on it. It seems a bit unpredictable and unreliable. A lot of folks who sing about it, don't seem to have it. Bad things happen to some people who do seem to have it. So my inclination has always been to work away, hoping to make enough friends and have enough success to satisfy.

Ted L. Estess

To tell the truth, Sam Southard's teaching strategy didn't work with me. I went to seminary in a slough of religious despond and personal negativity, and Southard's strategy didn't change much of that.

It should be said that Samuel Southard knew all about negativism, especially that which had been produced by southern evangelism; and all my friends, to different degrees, bore the effects of that blight upon the land. Southard thought that negativity—whether generated by evangelism or by something else, say, by one's parents or spouse—is so strong in our culture that nothing, literally nothing human, can mitigate it.

Of course there are sufficient reasons for any of us to be negative, but southern evangelism set me thinking about negativity in the wrong way. For one thing, southern evangelism placed self-negation right in the center of the "good news."

I think back to revival weeks, which were scheduled for twice a year, in the Baptist church in any southern town in the 1950s. The week started on a Sunday morning with friendly feelings toward ourselves and other folks. We rivaled the Rotarians in cheerfulness.

At seven in the morning and night for a week, nearly every Baptist in town gathered to sing those old songs. Everybody felt terrific with those lilting melodies and rhythms coursing through every drop of Baptist blood. The old songs did what music alone among all the arts can do: they *created*, at least for the time of our singing, not only the mood but also the meaning of that about which we sang.

By about Wednesday or Thursday night, I would be beaten down by the good news. By that time, the proclamation of the depravity of human beings had taken effect. What started out making me feel good ended up making me feel bad. The sad truth is that southern evangelism purported to provide the answer for a problem which it, in large part, had created: self-negation.

One night a group us young Baptists from Tylertown drove a hundred miles north to Jackson to attend a Billy Graham crusade. We got into the football stadium off North State Street and started singing. One song made us all feel real good. In 2/2 time, it had a bouncy rhythm and a rousing beat. All forty thousand tremulant souls in that stadium felt triumphant over the world as we howled at the top of our lungs: "Life now is sweet and my joy is complete for I am saved, saved"—and for the finale, those who could do so went up to high B-flat, screaming as loud as they could—"SAVED."

Forty thousand throats were hoarse when we finished that song. Everybody felt great. The back of my neck tingled with delight, my heart warmed to the core.

It didn't hold. By the time I walked from my seat on the thirty-five yard line out to the parking lot, I felt terrible. Driving back to Tylertown that night, I didn't have it, and I knew it. Others probably suspected as much of me.

Here I was: an Eagle Scout, a three-times All-Conference football player, a straight-A student, an Eagle scout, a winner of the Baptist Young People's Bible Sword Drill, a State 4-H Club Champion, captain of the Tylertown Blue Devils football team, a diligent piano player, the beloved son of loving parents, and a member of the Tylertown Youth Civil Defense Team that on Sunday afternoons looked out for enemy planes flying overhead, and a bust at getting good and saved.

The best analogy with a Baptist revival I know is a Texas Aggie football rally. One fine Friday this fervent Aggie pulls on his boots, gets a hair cut, washes his pick-up truck, and goes to the pep rally before the big game. He stands there and does all the yells, bursting them out at thirty-two decibels. The Aggie yell leaders light the bonfire, the flames of which reach for the heavens through the dark Texas sky. Then everybody sings the Aggie War Hymn, which is much like singing "I'm saved, saved," and at the top of your lungs, "SAVED."

But then the Aggies lose the game, 48 to zip. What had made our Aggie feel great now makes him feel terrible. He cut his hair and washed his truck for nothing.

Whether in the Baptist revival or the Aggie pep rally, the psychological operations seem, at least on the surface, similar. Both gatherings generate a fervent and delicious, though temporary, inflation of isolated individuals. Aided by stirring music and exalted words—which, as music is wont to do, bypasses the cerebral censors and works directly on the emotions—many inflated individuals meld into one grander, transcendent self. But this grander, transcendent self inevitably is deflated as the effects of the music and the exalted words slowly dissipate in the night air.

A good deal of my youth was spent cutting my hair, washing my truck, and going to Baptist pep rallies. I learned all the songs, even how to play them on the piano and organ. I gave up dancing; tried not to pleasure myself; read the Bible twice a day; said prayers morning and night. It didn't work, at least not like I thought it should. It didn't hold.

Miss Maggie Simmons would be especially downcast to hear this news. Miss Maggie was vigorous in her efforts in behalf of young souls in the Tylertown Baptist Church. She seemed to have been born about the time Mississippi became a state, which was 1817. She was still going strong in 1952 as the sponsor of the Royal Ambassadors group. She was interested in all of us boys becoming missionaries and going out to save others, especially children in Africa, the same children who would not be allowed in our church if they were lucky enough to get saved. She taught us the Royal Ambassadors' song, which we sang at our meeting every Monday afternoon: "I am a stranger here, my home is far away upon a golden shore."

Now, you tell me, what business does a group of ten-year-old boys in Tylertown, Mississippi, have singing, "My home is far away upon a golden shore"?

Somewhere between those Monday afternoons and my arrival in Lousiville, Kentucky, I had decided to pay attention to my home close by, which is what I've been doing ever since. At some point, I was no longer able, at least with the naiveté, of a child, fervently to sing, "This world is not my home, I'm just a-traveling through." I had come to see that before getting into the home beyond the sea, I had first to learn to be at home on *terra firma*.

By the time I studied theology, I had long since stopped bothering whether I was saved or not. But the mark of evangelical negativism remained with me. It was like a brand on an old horse: a horse can be twenty years old but the brand burned on his butt when he was a yearling lingers on. It may be overgrown with scar tissue and hair, but it's there, an identifying mark. So it was with me: I carried negativism like a brand on my butt.

Sam Southard's efforts to move his students beyond the branding that they had received from southern evangelism didn't work. The approach was too austere. It depended on a God who seemed to have gone on holiday. Perhaps I had seen too many Bergman movies to be a good candidate for my good teacher's strategy.

I would have preferred a gentler path, and perhaps would have benefited from a more affirmative approach, religiously and personally. I needed human mediators of amazing grace, but Southard didn't allow for any. He believed that human mediators do not mediate amazing grace: they largely mediate their own projections and perverse expectations and desires. If you don't believe that, try being married to the same person for twenty or thirty years: you'll spend half the time working through the projections, expectations, and desires that your spouse lays on you. And the last thing you want, Southard thought, is for a wife to depend on her husband for her ultimate well-being, and vice versa, or for parents so to depend on their children. That's a recipe for disaster if ever there was one. Furthermore, why should we depend ultimately on any other person? He or she is bound to be as fragile, vulnerable, needy, and, in fundamental ways, as unreliable as we.

Somewhere Franz Kafka wrote, "What is laid upon us is to accomplish the negative. The positive is already given." That's what Southard was doing: accomplishing, or realizing, or intensifying the negative. What I never really heard from him was the other part, the part about the positive being given, being already there, even before the question of whether it is there arises in the first place. I'm sure he said it. I'm sure he enacted it. I just didn't get it.

So instead of leading me out of the negativity that was the legacy of my early religious formation, my teacher led me deeper into it. He intensified the negative all right, but the release of the positive never came. Seeking to heal, he delivered another wound.

Late one winter afternoon during my last year in Louisville, I walked from the library over for an appointment with Professor Southard. On the way across that vast playing field, a bird flew overhead. Doing what birds do, he shat. His dropping plopped on my shoulder. It was during that meeting that Southard, somewhat to my surprise, was to advise me to get out the South to go to graduate school. But I wasn't thinking about graduate school when I walked in: I was thinking about bird shit on my new corduroy jacket.

Sitting down, I halfway jokingly suggested to Southard that being shat on was a parable. It was a real and visible sign of my equally real and invisible negativism. Southard smiled, confirming me in the negative.

But he might have said, "My young friend, that bird is trying to wake you up. You're not paying attention to things, many of them good, all around you. And you yourself have gifts and should be grateful for them. I want you to enjoy yourself. I insist on it, and I am your teacher. Walk on this campus as though every one of those Beech trees was planted with you in mind, because it was. Never give yourself over to gratuitous absolutes, especially negative ones. Fight despair as if your life depends on it, because it does. I insist on it, and I am your teacher. As best you can, avoid living on borrowed pain: you'll have enough of your own. Now get out of here and go have a good time. I insist on it, and I am your teacher."

Since being a teacher is something like being a parent, you don't know how you're doing until it's too late. So I don't blame Sam Southard. He was like Miss Maggie Simmons, doing what he could. I'm grateful to them both. If they had not taught me what they did, I never would have learned in other ways what I need. They did what all teachers do to students: wound them. In time, if we are lucky, we come to love our wounds.

It has taken the best part of my life, but I've come 'round to honoring, if not always loving, the wounding I received at the hands of southern evangelism, which is, of course, really part of coming 'round to being capable of enjoying myself and of receiving whatever regard others might have for me. It's a part of coming home to, and coming home by way of, my own story. That's amazing, grace, too.

## Mint Juleps in January

When I arrived in Syracuse, Manny would hardly give me the time of day. The quintessential New Yorker, Harry Weintraub, was irrepressible and connecting with everyone, even a Mississippian like me, but that fellow Manny turned away.

Then one day just as the second semester was starting, Manny happened to overhear Weintraub mocking my accent and asking me, "Mister Ted, did y'all have a ni-icce time down there in Miz-sip ovah Chrees-mass, you and Miz Sybil? I'm sho glad y'all made it back he-ah safe and sound."

That was all it took. Manny—I forget his last name—latched on to me like I was somebody. "Are you from Mississippi?" he asked, his eyes bright.

"Yes, I'm originally from Mississippi," I replied. I was uneasy with this questioning, because I was uneasy being from Mississippi. I assumed most folks assumed I must be a cracker, a redneck, a hick. Weintraub mocked my way of talking, but always in good fun. He was like my students. In the dormitory, they would put on their Southern drawl and say, "You in Colonel Estess' class, ain't you? That Colonel Estess is all-rite." I enjoyed that, because the students were enjoying themselves enjoying me. And I liked being called Colonel Estess.

"Where in Mississippi?" This fellow is persistent, I thought.

"A little town in south Mississippi," I said, "about ninety miles north of New Orleans. Its name is Tylertown, but we pronounce it Tarlertown."

"Ninety miles north of Nawleens," he replied, trying to speak the name like a native of the Crescent City. "Do you know that Judah P. Benjamin was from Nawleens?"

"No, I don't think so." I didn't tell Manny that I didn't know who Judah P. Benjamin was. Never heard of him.

"You know who Judah P. Benjamin was, don't you?" he asked again. He glared at me as though I was on trial. His eyes dilated behind his glasses, and he leaned up toward me to look me straight in the eye.

"No," I said, "I guess I don't know who Judah P. Benjamin was. I don't think I've heard of Judah P. Benjamin." I really didn't appreciate the interrogation.

"I can't believe it." Now he was all but shouting. "I really cannot believe it." I'm not sure if anyone else saw it or not, but this stout fellow from Jersey City levitated right there in the seminar room in the Religion Department of Syracuse University. Here he was up above me now, about a foot taller than I, his eyes bulging and peering down at me, threatening, accusing. Frankly, I was frightened.

The only other time I had ever seen anyone levitate was when my brother came home one day and told me that he had had a good, long look into the Tylertown High School Lady Blue Devils' dressing room after basketball practice. He was stout too and his eyes dilated and he rose about a foot off the floor, but he didn't peer down at me. His eyes were unfocussed, as though he had entered another realm.

"You are a Mississippian, a son of the Confederacy, and you don't know who Judah P. Benjamin was?" Manny's voice boomed all through the religion offices. A secretary stuck her head out to see what was going on. I don't think anyone fully understood what was happening. I know I didn't.

"Well, you come to my apartment on Saturday night," he said sharply. "I'll tell you who Judah P. Benjamin was. You know what day Saturday is, don't you?" I felt bad telling Manny that I didn't know what day Saturday was, but things were better now that both of his feet were back on the floor.

I don't recall who all was there for the party. Weintraub was, I'm sure, as was a fellow named Frank who was trying hard to be a philosopher. I told Frank that I was surprised to see him. Sybil and I had already been to his house one night that semester for a visit. He was married to a woman who was about ten years older than he. Frank was working on Kant.

At Baylor in that long, hot summer of 1964, I had written a paper on a small section of Kant's *Critique of Pure Reason*; but, to tell the truth, I hardly understood a word of what Kant wrote or of what I wrote about what he wrote. About the only thing I knew with some degree of clarity about Kant was a story that my teacher Professor Hopper told. I figured he liked it because I heard him tell it four or five times that first year in Syracuse. Every day at the same time there in Königsberg, the great philosopher would take his walk. One day, he happened to see a neighbor woman tending her garden, and he stopped to speak. "Meine Frau," Kant said, "your garden is very small." The neighbor woman replied, "Yes, Herr Professor Kant, it's small down here, but it's miles high, it's miles high."

He didn't know it yet, but Kant was miles too high for that little fellow named Frank. In another three or four years, he found out, and ended up a financial planner in Buffalo.

That night in Frank's apartment, we had been sitting for a while, just visiting, when Frank mentioned how important his work was and how he soon was going to make a major contribution to Kant studies. All the time he was talking, I was feeling worse and worse. I just wanted to get through graduate school. I didn't know what I was going to write my dissertation on and here was a fellow who was already making a major contribution.

"And you know, I work on Kant all the time," Frank said, his voice lowering to indicate the seriousness of the matter, "all the time, day and night, work on Kant—it's all I do, all I want to do."

His wife, platinum blond she was, nodded in agreement. "That's right," she said. "That's all Frank does, all he wants to do, night and day, is work on Kant. I ask him all the time, 'Frank, honey, don't you want to do something tonight besides work on Kant?' Every night he says that's all he wants to do, so I just let him do it."

"Tonight," Frank continued, "I really should be spending this time thinking about what I am going to write tomorrow."

Not a single person in Tarlertown, Mississippi, would ever think of saying any such thing to guests, even for so important a matter as working on Immanuel Kant. So I thought of replying, "Well, *excuusse* me," and getting up and walking out the door. But being new to the Deep North, I said, "That's right, Frank, if you are going to do important work, you must give Kant your full attention." When Sybil and I left, I told her that I thought Frank was a pompous ass and ill-mannered, too, telling us that he ought to be doing something else after he was the one who invited us to dinner in the first place. Sybil allowed how she thought I had been a pompous ass myself and that Frank and I had left her and his wife out of the conversation and that she was about ready to decide that all graduates students were pompous asses. I really couldn't disagree with her.

But as Manny met us at the door on Saturday night, he was as gracious as gracious could be. Sybil whispered in my ear, "He's nothing like what you said. He's charming."

I had to admit I hadn't experienced such charm since I left Mississippi. Perhaps Syracuse, New York, wouldn't be as bereft of social grace as I had feared.

Then I noticed the music quietly playing in the room. My heart warmed to a familiar old tune, and I am sure I caught the warm scent of Magnolia blossoms and sweet Honeysuckle. Softly, underneath the chatter of a room full of graduate students in religion, the words of the old song broke through:

> Oh, I wish I was in the land of cotton,
> Old times there are not forgotten,
> Look away, Look away,
> Look away, Dixieland.

I didn't recognize the singer. Maybe it was Willie Nelson, but I could clearly hear the words beneath the chatter:

> Away, away, away
> Down South, in Dixie.

Manny ushered Sybil and me through the crowd. He acted as though we were the long awaited guests of honor. I was feeling better and better at this party on Saturday night, January 19th, 1969. Manny passed us from guest to guest, being sure that we had proper introductions. "Have you met my good friends, Sybil and Ted Estess?" he asked. "Sybil and Ted are from Mississippi, you know. You didn't? Well, they are. Born and raised right there both of them, right down there in Old Miz-sip."

I really didn't know what was going on. I felt bad about being from Mississippi, and here this fellow Manny was carrying on like Sybil and I possessed some special charisma precisely because we were from Mississippi.

I can remember in my life only one fellow telling me that he wished he was from Mississippi. When I say I am from Mississippi, most folks seem relieved. "Thank God," they whisper under their breath, "at least I'm not from Mississippi."

We were sitting on the floor at my house in Houston and I was talking to a fellow named Rust Hills. Rust Hills was the fiction editor of *Esquire* magazine at the time, and he asked me where I was from. He was there with his wife, the writer Joy Williams, who had given a reading at the university. We were having a little party in her honor.

"Where are you from?" Rust Hills asked. I felt, as I always felt back then, a little uneasy telling a sophisticated fellow like Rust Hills where I am from. But I had to answer, and I couldn't say San Francisco.

"I'm from Mississippi, originally," I said. I added *originally* in order to suggest that I had, many years ago, moved on from that state of deprivation. It's like what that doctor's wife said to Sybil a couple of months ago when Sybil told her she had lived in Syracuse and Montana and various other places and had been living in Houston for many years. "But I'm originally from Mississippi," Sybil added. To which the doctor's wife replied, "Well, you sure have come up in the world."

But Rust Hills said, "I've always wanted to be from Mississippi."

If I hadn't been sitting down already, I'm sure I would have fallen over, right there in my living room on Faculty Lane. Here was a sophisticated man, the fiction editor of *Esquire* magazine, straight from New York City, sitting on my living room floor and looking me straight in the eye and telling me what no man has told me before or since, saying as clear as crystal, "I've always wanted to be from Mississippi," as though being from Mississippi were a privilege instead of a mark of ignorance, constitutional lawlessness, and bigotry. He wasn't drunk, either.

"Actually, there are two places," Rust Hill continued, "only two, that I've always wanted to be from, Brooklyn and Mississippi." Then he added—at least I think he added—"But I was born in New Jersey."

Strangely, I found myself replying, "That's too bad, Rust, you being from New Jersey. Mississippi is a great place to be from."

Perhaps that night in Syracuse Manny felt like he was working under a disability similar to Rust Hill's, both of them being from New Jersey.

As we moved around the room, Manny wanted to know if Sybil and I had made the Pilgrimage to Natchez and whether we had walked the battlefield at Vicksburg. He was pleased that I had done both, but disappointed that Sybil hadn't yet seen the battlefield.

We had by now moved through the crowd when Manny herded us toward his bedroom. "I want to tell you about Judah P. Benjamin," he said. "You two are from Mississippi, you need to know."

Manny led us into his bedroom, which seemed more like a sanctuary than an ordinary room. On the walls, even in the dim light, I could make out the figures in the framed prints. There was Stonewall Jackson, dignified, a brilliant strategist and a man of prayer. Next to him was J. E. B. Stuart, resplendent in the gray. And there was Nathan Bedford Forrest, astride one of the three horses shot—as I had always heard the story—from beneath him on a single day, charging behind the Union lines at Shiloh, entering thereby the mythic realm, such doomed glory purchased at such doomed a price.

We approached the high altar at the end of the room. On a table there was a cake, extending the full length and width of the table and ready for the guests later on. I thought Manny might be expecting me to salute, for the cake was decorated to show the Stars and Bars, the battle flag of the Confederacy. Behind the cake there were two candles, one on each side of the centerpiece of the altar. Looking up, I stared into the sad, weary eyes of Robert E. Lee.

"What do folks down in Mississippi say about General Lee?" Manny asked. "Don't y'all say he's the greatest man who ever lived? That's what y'all say, isn't it?"

"Yes, Manny," I said, "that what some folks say down in Mississippi. They say that Robert E. Lee is the greatest man who ever lived next to Jesus Christ."

"Well, I think y'all ought to wish General Lee a happy birthday. It's General Lee's 162nd birthday, you know. He was born in Virginia on January 19th, 1807. He's 162 years old today. I'm surprised y'all didn't remember that, coming from Mississippi. We gonna sing Happy Birthday to the General later on when we cut the cake."

"Well, Manny," I said, "it just slipped my mind. I'm glad you reminded me." I didn't tell Manny that when I was a boy in Mississippi Jefferson Davis' birthday, not Robert E. Lee's, was a state holiday. After all, the President, though born in Kentucky, was a U.S. Senator from Mississippi and spent his last years down on the Coast at Beauvoir.

# Fishing Spirit Lake

All the time, Miz Sybil stood in silence. I knew she was mortified. What faint nostalgia I had for the Confederacy, even that displeased her. Sybil didn't think Robert E. Lee was the greatest man who ever lived next to Jesus Christ. She didn't even know who Traveler was. And here we were in a nut house with a deranged Yankee who had made his apartment into a shrine to Saint Robert E. Lee.

I don't know which is more disconcerting, to meet the strange in a strange place or to meet the familiar in a strange place. You expect the first: you go to a strange place and you expect to be surprised, shocked, to encounter something new. In this situation the strange is actually familiar, precisely because it meets your expectation that it will be strange.

But when you meet the familiar in a strange place and in a strange way, you are caught off guard. In that situation what you know as familiar is rendered strange. You thereby lose the anchor of the familiar against which you can judge something as strange. You feel like a child cast fresh and alone into the world. I was familiar with Robert E. Lee and Stonewall Jackson. But meeting them in an apartment in a dismal part of Syracuse, New York, on a wintry night in 1969, rendered them completely strange. I didn't know who they were any more.

It was something like what I had experienced a few years before when I spent three months in Japan. I had been sent over by Texas Baptist students to do some evangelizing and to meet with some already converted Japanese students. Week after week, I went to Japanese churches and heard familiar old Southern gospel songs being sung, in Japanese, mind you. On some occasions I even played the piano for the singing. There I was in a small, wooden church in Fujisawa, playing the piano for Japanese to sing a gospel song as familiar as my right hand.

> There is power, power,
> Wonder working power,
> In the blood of the Lamb.
> There is power, power,
> Wonder working power,
> In the precious blood of the Lamb.

As I listened to this old song in Japanese, it was rendered strange, even alien. It lost its familiarity forever. Before, I thought I knew what it meant. Since then, I've never been sure. In Syracuse on the night of

January 19th, 1969, I experienced something like that with Robert E. Lee.

Before Sybil could escape from the high altar and rejoin the other guests, Manny elbowed us to the right and brought us face to face with another photograph on the wall. "And *that*," Manny announced, "*that* is Judah P. Benjamin."

And sure enough, there was a photograph of a 19th-century gentleman, replete with long coat and watch fob, beard and long hair. He stood behind and to the side of an empty chair. His right hand rested on the back. His eyes had a determined look, resigned and resolute, and firm to the task.

It was obvious I ought to know who this fellow was standing before an empty chair and hanging there on the wall before my very eyes, but I didn't. I wanted to ask, "Manny, who is Judah P. Benjamin?" But I couldn't bring myself to do it.

"Who is Judah P. Benjamin?" Sybil asked.

I thought Manny would come out of his beard. He snorted like a dragon. "It's amazing, really amazing," he said. "You don't know, Sybil? Really, you don't know who Judah P. Benjamin is?"

"No, Manny," Sybil replied. "I don't know who Judah P. Benjamin is. I've never heard of Judah P. Benjamin. Who is Judah P. Benjamin?"

"Judah P. Benjamin was the Secretary of State of the Confederacy," Manny announced, and as he straightened his pudgy frame, I thought for a second that I saw him, just for a second, levitate again, not as high as earlier in the week, but up to where he could look Sybil in the eye.

"Judah P. Benjamin was President Jefferson Davis' Secretary of State. He was almost made Vice President. But Jefferson asked him to be Secretary of State. He was from Nawleens. And"—here Manny paused, and with a jerk of the hand, he announced—"*and* he was *Jewish*."

I hope I did not insult our host that night but I really didn't know how to react. What I was supposed to say?

I didn't know at the time that Manny was Jewish. There weren't any Jews in Tylertown, Mississippi; so never having known any Jews, I had never thought to wonder whether or not a person were Jewish. Maybe that would have helped, would have given me a clue of how to proceed, what to do. I could have said, "I don't know much about Jewish participation in the War Between the States." Maybe that would have been a polite response. I could have asked, "What part did Jews play in the War, Manny?" I could even have put three syllables in the word "waa-ah-hrr."

But standing before this photograph of a man I had never heard of, and being confronted for the first time with the fact that Judah P. Benjamin was the first Jewish Secretary of State of the Confederacy, I didn't know which way to turn. I didn't want to be impolite, whatever I said or did. Walker Percy is right in saying that the South has given two things to the country: good cooking and good manners. I don't cook much, so I always try to be well mannered.

Later on, I began to surmise that maybe Manny, a kid growing up there in Hoboken, had just felt left out. He didn't have all that much going for him. Couldn't play baseball, wasn't exceptionally smart. He was Jewish, and that could have been enough, but he didn't know much about Judaism and few of his friends took it seriously. So by an incongruous stroke of imaginative ingenuity, he enlarged himself by glomming onto the Confederacy as a source of mythic enhancement, somehow legitimating his Confederate sympathies by emphasizing, as far as I know, the most noteworthy point of Jewish participation in the ill-fated, yet (to Manny) glorious and doomed affair.

So faced with the photograph of Judah P. Benjamin, I was like Moses before the burning bush. I had nothing to say. Manny helped me out. "Now here," he said, reaching over to take a sheath of papers from the shelf, "here is some information about Judah P. Benjamin. I put this together and I want y'all to have a copy. Y'all are from Mississippi and need to know about Judah P. Benjamin."

We moved back toward the party going strong in the living room. Weintraub was there, stroking his beard and regaling against Nixon and the Vietnam War. Two nuns—who were also grad students in religion and the first nuns I had ever met in my life—were giggling at Weintraub's outrageous hilarity. It all seemed like a lot of fun, but Sybil and I didn't linger long enough to eat a slice of the Stars and Bars and sing Happy Birthday to General Lee. Sybil said she wasn't feeling very well and I was a little disoriented myself. Fortunately, Manny was soon up to his knees in mint juleps and hardly noticed, so we maintained social grace, leaving early like we did. It was the last time I drank mint juleps in January.

Easing along on the dark ice on the sidewalk toward our car, I suddenly felt that I didn't know where I was. I was afraid I was going to fall. It had happened once before that first winter in Syracuse. I was walking back to my car on campus at the university, walking along through the first snowstorm of my life. I wasn't sure where the car was. I couldn't see ahead. I would have returned to the religion department, but I was sure I couldn't find my way back there. I thought I would fall down and die in the snow before I found the car. I leaned into the wind howling off Onondaga Lake and full of blistering snow. Later, when I got to our apartment on Wetzel Road, Sybil came in the door and told me that she had thought she was not going to make it from school. Walking through the snow just two hundred yards from her classroom to our living room, she had become disoriented and unsure of the way. She said she felt lost and disoriented.

That's the way I felt leaving that party that night: I was in a strange place with strange people and I wasn't sure I was going to make it home.

Fishing Spirit Lake

# A Picture Holds Us Captive
## I

Toward the end of my second year in Syracuse I worked up a presentation on Picasso for one of Professor David Miller's seminars. I didn't know much about Picasso, but of course that did not deter me. That's one reason Syracuse was good for me: I spent a fair amount of time talking about things I didn't know much about. There is no better preparation for being a teacher than that.

For weeks I studied a series of etchings that Picasso made in the 1920s. The etchings were of a child and the Minotaur. I was interested in the child back then, never having been one myself. You remember the Minotaur, that mythological creature with the body of a man and the head of a bull that lived in the labyrinth beneath King Minos' Palace on the island of Crete.

In early May I came to make my presentation to the seminar. "Here we see the child and the Minotaur," I said to Miller and my fellow students, pointing them to the slide on the screen. "Notice the young girl on the ladder and the Minotaur below. The child is going up the ladder with her light, in flight from the threatening Minotaur at the foot of the ladder." I went on to associate the Minotaur with sexual energy and the young girl with innocence and vulnerability. I talked about prepubescent flight from chaos and darkness and sexuality and death and other happy subjects.

Finally, I shut up, and Professor Miller asked his first question. "Mr. Estess, why do you think that the child is going up the ladder? You could as easily say the child is going down the ladder."

I was undone. To hide my panic, I turned to look at the slide on the screen. He was right. Any fool could see it. The child could as easily be going down the ladder as up the ladder. Why hadn't I seen that? I had been looking at those etchings for three months. I had read everything there was to read about those etchings. None of the experts had said anything about the child going *down* the ladder. That would change everything. It would be like Daniel stepping into the lion's den. Who would think that Daniel would stand down a lion? Who would think a child would go toward a Minotaur? But, indeed, Picasso's child holds the light in her hand, and could be taking light into the labyrinth and toward the great bull.

Turning back to the seminar, I was face to face with a Great Bull. I was the child and my light was nearly out. I wanted to flee, and would have if I had been near the door. I was exposed. I knew that my teacher and my classmates were on to me: I didn't know what I was talking about, and they knew it. For twenty-two years, I had been in school: that was all I had ever done, go to school, twelve years in Missssippi, four in Texas, another four in Kentucky, and now two in New York. For twenty-two years, I had fooled people in every school and in four states. From Mississippi to Texas to Kentucky to New York, I had kept my secret. Now it was established beyond a reasonable doubt, and brought out in the open for the whole fricking world to see: Estess doesn't know rat shit. What would I tell my parents?

Miller asked a second question. "Mr. Estess, what makes you think the child is a young girl? It's not clear," he added, "whether the child is a girl or a boy, is it? Picasso could be dealing with androgyny, you know."

I didn't half know what androgyny is, and I sure didn't have anything to say about it that afternoon. I wanted to go home. But I did have sense enough to see that if I had learned anything, it had little to do with Picasso. Picasso's etchings had been the occasion, not the content of what I had learned.

On the way out of the seminar room, my teacher stopped to talk to me. Now that he knew how stupid I was, I had figured he never would speak to me again. He would recommend that I be dismissed from the program. "Ted," he said, "you might remember that aphorism from Wittgenstein."

I wasn't sure what an aphorism is, but I did know Wittgenstein— well, I had read some of Ludwig Wittgenstein, that great and notoriously complex Viennese philosopher of the first half of the twentieth-century.

"What's that, Professsor Miller?" I asked.

He replied, "A picture holds us captive—and will not let us go."

I walked out of the room and across the campus, repeating those words again and again like a mantra, breathing in and breathing out, "A picture holds us captive—and will not let us go. A picture holds us captive—and will not let us go. A picture . . . ."

That spring while I was studying Picasso, a picture of Picasso's picture held me captive and would not let me go. I could see only my picture, the one in which the girl was going up the ladder; consequently, I couldn't see what was right before my nose. I couldn't attend to it. My picture held me captive and would not let me go. The child might be going down the ladder. In order to see what was before his eyes, the captive needed to be set free.

As much as anything, that is what I got out of graduate study at Syracuse University: I was released, at least in part, from a few of the pictures that had held me captive. I got unhooked. Maybe that, I thought one day, is why my teacher in Kentucky insisted that I go north to study: he knew I needed to get unhooked.

But to tell the truth, getting unhooked is not altogether a good thing, and it took me the best part of several decades to recover. I am glad it happened to me when I was young. It is not good for a man my age never to have been unhooked, but neither is it good for a person forever to remain so.

Another thing that came out of Syracuse is that I met a passel of interesting people, some pretty famous ones too, all of whom had pictures to exhibit. I stood around at David Miller's house talking to Joseph Campbell and Rollo May, Alan Watts and Huston Smith, Sam Keen and Norman O. Brown, Hans George Gadamer and Amos Wilder, and the like. Getting to know folks like that teaches you pretty quickly that they are about as messed up as everybody else.

One day I was able to have lunch with Alan Watts. Watts was an Episcopalian priest who turned Zen Buddhist back in the 1950s and wrote a book. Over the next twenty-five years he wrote twenty-five more books, but it was always the same book with a different title. As I said, Watts turned Zen Buddhist and wrote a book. That semester, Miller and I were teaching some Buddhism to a class, and we decided to show an Alan Watts film. As a climax to the course, Watts himself would come to town and lecture for us.

Our first problem was which Watts film to show. The university film library had three, so Miller and I went over to the film library and screened all three. We couldn't choose among them. They were like Watt's books: the same film with a different title. Miller suggested that we show all three at the same time. We would have three projectors sitting in the middle of the lecture hall, with one showing one film toward the front, and the other two projecting on the walls to the side. One sound track would be heard.

It was crazy, but it worked, which is to say that the kaleidoscope of images that surrounded the students was a perfect match for the kaleidoscopic shifting of images that was going on in their minds. In front and to the sides, the room was suffused with images of autumn leaves falling into mountain streams, and birds sitting on snowy branches, and clouds scuttling across mountain peaks, and all the while we heard Alan Watts' sonorous voice, "All is turning and drifting, through endless time, as one thing flows into another, becomes another, is another, as snow falls and leaves drift, across and down into the ocean at the foot of the mountain, and at the center of all that is, you see, suddenly you see the light turn to shadow, become the shadow, as day gives way to night, and night to day," and all the while, we sat with two hundred anxious undergraduates as images flickered around us, images of leaves and snow and birds on frosty branches, with Watts' droning on, "and you see, suddenly you see what you knew all the time, the light turn to shadow, become the shadow, as day gives way to night, and night to day."

Leaving the lecture hall that day and turning on to sidewalks covered with the sludge of a late March snowfall, the undergraduates were chirping like birds on a frosty branch. "That is the best class I've ever been to," one young fellow opined to another, his scruffy vest festooned with peace signs and various other symbols of counter-cultural neglect. "Nothing like it, man, nothing like it," came the reply. I felt pleased myself, walking along with Doug Gunn, another faculty member teaching in the class.

Stepping outside the building, Gunn and I walked over to the Commons in front of Hendricks Chapel to watch an anti-war rally going on. It was an early spring day in 1970, and Dick Gregory was there to talk about ending the war and eating right. After he pretty much gave up being a comedian, Dick Gregory spent his time on two things: war and eating right.

"Let me read you what I've got in my wallet," Dick shouted. "I carry it with me all the time." Doug Gunn and I were sitting on the top step of the stately chapel, a good seventy-five yards away from Dick and his crowd, but the loudspeakers brought every word to us, even as we chatted away.

That was years before Dick Gregory went into eating right full time. On one occasion, he took special interest in a young man on Long Island named Walter Hudson. One day, Walter went to the bathroom in his house and got stuck coming out the door. Walter weighed 1197 pounds. His mother called in the carpenters, and they came and took out the door so Walter could get back to bed and eat some more hamburgers. He was exhausted by it all.

Dick Gregory heard about Walter and flew in from his home down on an island off of Cuba to help out if he could. Dick went on TV with Walter, and Walter said that all he wanted to do in life was to lose enough weight to be able to get out the front door. Walter said he appreciated Mr. Gregory coming up from his island to help him and he was going to do what Mr. Gregory said. He wasn't going to eat three dozen Twinkies and two boxes of sausages a day any more. He was going to eat sprouts and drink Mr. Gregory's tea.

And he did. After six months on sprouts and Dick's tea, Walter lost 247 pounds. He got out the front door of his house for the first time in six years. For that special day, Dick Gregory came up from his island again and went back on TV with Walter. I watched the two of them standing on the front porch, Dick and Walter, busting their buttons with pride. Dick said it was quite an accomplishment, Walter's being able to get out the front door for the first time in six years.

But it didn't last. Walter got hooked again on hamburgers, sausages, and Twinkies. Dick made the long trek up to Long Island to see what he could do. Dick said to Walter, "Look, man, you already lost 247 pounds. Can't you hold out, man?"

But now that I think about it, what is 247 pounds to an 1197-pound man?

Finally, Dick went on TV, this time by himself. He said that he reluctantly was withdrawing his help from Mr. Hudson. Yes, it was true, he said to the reporters, Mr. Hudson was now back up to two boxes of sausages and three dozen Twinkies a day and he wasn't drinking the tea. Dick said he was just going to go on back down to his island and leave Mr. Hudson to make it on his own. He had done what he could. I always appreciated that about Dick: he did what he could.

But all that was a long time after Doug Gunn and I were listening to Dick Gregory admonishing the crowd in front of Hendricks Chapel that spring day of 1970. There must have been a thousand students in scruffy jeans out there, taking in Dick's words about the war like they were Twinkies and hamburgers.

"I want you to carry a copy with you all the time, like I do," Dick shouted. "Here it is. Folded up, right here." Dick held up a frayed piece of paper and began to read to the cheers of the crowd. He read, "When in the course of human events, it becomes necessary for one people to dissolve the political bonds," and the way cheers erupted across the Commons, it crossed my mind that perhaps these students had never heard these words before.

"See all these buildings," Doug Gunn said to me.

"What about them?" I asked.

"We hold these truths to be self-evident, that all men are created equal. . . ."

"Take a good look at these buildings," Gunn said, moving his arm around and pointing to the mottled collection of buildings surrounding the Commons at Syracuse University. Gunn was an assistant professor with a Ph.D. from Yale. He was what I have come to call an "eschatophile," a lover of the end, an "eschatophiliac." In that, he was not much different from Dick Gregory and lots of other people. Contemporary society is filled with eschatophiliacs. An eschatophiliac is someone proclaiming that the end will surely come if other folks keep on doing whatever it is that they are doing. The fundamental message of an eschatophiliac is, "Whatever you are doing, stop it." In Doug Gunn's case, he was convinced, I suppose, that all the counter-cultural upheaval of the age heralded a radical dismantling of the fundamental institutions of the society. That's the picture that held him captive.

# Fishing Spirit Lake

"But when a long train of abuses and usurpations, pursuing invariably the same object, evinces a design to reduce them under absolute despotism...." The roar of the students made it hard for me to hear Gunn.

"Take a good look at these buildings," he said. "They won't be standing long. Stone by stone, brick by brick, they will come tumbling down. It will happen in our lifetime, well within our lifetime. Like Joshua and Jericho, you wait and see."

"It is their right, it is their duty, to throw off such government, and to provide new guards for their future security." In the distance, the crowd went into a frenzy. I looked around at the buildings surrounding the Commons, wondering when the stones might come tumbling down.

A few weeks later Alan Watts came to town to lecture to the class, but before the lecture, David Miller and I and a couple of other faculty members met him at a country club for lunch. Watts had had a bad night in Pittsburgh, where he had stopped over to try to get his son out of jail. It seemed as though Watts had been up all night talking to the cops and to the D. A.'s office and to lawyers. This was revealed as Watts ordered his second double martini, Beefeater's, straight up, with a twist.

"Sons of bitches," Watts said, "they could have left that boy alone," and we all commiserated with him over our Reuben sandwiches. Watts didn't eat a bite.

Back in the lecture hall, the students waited to hear Alan Watts. A hush fell over the room as we walked in from the club. I felt proud, striding down the aisle behind Alan Watts and David Miller and Doug Gunn to take a seat in the front. Miller did the introduction. As with all Miller's introductions, that one was long. It thus served as something of an insurance policy against a bad lecture: in case Watts had nothing to say, the audience wouldn't leave empty-handed.

"And please join me," Miller finally came to say, "in welcoming a person whom I have known for many years, someone whom we have all been looking forward to hearing, my friend, Alan Watts." With that, Miller turned toward Alan Watts, who sat partially hidden behind the lectern. From my seat, I had been watching it all. During the introduction, Watts the Zen practitioner had closed his eyes and started to meditate, composing himself for the words of wisdom he was about to speak, centering himself, listening to the silence within so that he could speak to the silent ones without. I admired him, sitting there, meditating, focused, the centered one amid the decentering distractions of the day.

"I present to you Alan Watts," Miller repeated, "my good friend, Alan Watts." By then a meditative calm held poor Watts captive. The martinis and the all-nighter in the Pittsburgh jail had done their work: he was sound asleep. "Alan. Alan." Miller said off-mike. Watts jerked to attention and took the mike from Miller, and as he began to speak, familiar sonorous tones suffused the room, "All is turning and drifting, through endless time, and one thing flows into another, becomes another, is another," and within the mind's eye of each person in the hall, pictures of drifting snow and falling leaves and flowing water and floating birds moved toward the sea.

As I walked out of the lecture room with Doug Gunn, the students were chirping like birds on a snowy branch. "Wasn't that wonderful?" one girl from Poughkeepsie asked me. "Yes," I said, "I suppose it was."

# II

Today when I think of persons being held by a picture, I think of my father. He's into his eighties now and doing pretty well. Sometimes he gets sad. One of his brothers, Wensel by name, is dying with cancer in Florida. Cancer took off Smith, another of his brothers, last November. His brother Vardaman died several years ago. Another brother named Lynn broke his neck in a diving accident in 1925. My father helped pull him out of the water.

My father is working a good deal at something that we religion students talked about in our seminars at Syracuse University. We talked about "perspectival" thinking, about seeing, and about what we—following a philosopher named Ludwig Binswanger—called "as-if-thinking." My father talks about the same thing, but he uses words such as "attitude" and "disposition" and "keeping things in perspective." He'll say, "I have to remember I've had a good life. The Lord has been mighty good to me and your mother."

My father is working to hold on hard to a picture. He is the better every day for it, more grateful, usually more cheerful, and better able to stay the course. He's more pleasant and helpful to my mother as well, all because of the picture that holds him captive day to day. Following Wallace Stevens—a poet that we paid a lot of attention to at Syracuse—one could say that the Christian picture is my father's "supreme fiction," though he of course would not know what I mean in talking that way. I figure my father will be able to hold up to the end if he can hold on to that picture and see the world as if it really were that way.

By the time I finished graduate school at Syracuse University in the spring of 1971, I was holding on hard to not holding on to pictures. That was my picture: not having a picture. By "picture" here, I mean a *big* picture, a comprehensive or encompassing way of looking at reality and at the world. Examples of encompassing pictures include Christianity, existentialism, Judaism, Freudianism, Americanism, Scientism, and the like. A friend of mine speaks of such pictures with the acronym GUNS—Grand Unifying Narratives. He told me not long ago that he prefers PINS—Personal Individual Narratives of the sort that I am given to tell.

Still, coming out of graduate school, I could talk about lots of GUNS, but didn't hold to any one. Not one held me. I appreciated them all, without favoring any one over any other. I sometimes looked down on folks who did.

All that it great, it really is, if you can keep it up and hold it in perspective, and if you can keep your sense of humor. But I sometimes think that holding on hard to not holding on to a picture is like Walter Hudson the 1197-pound man trying to live on sprouts and Dick Gregory's tea. Sprouts and Dick Gregory's tea are nothing to an 1197-pound man. Anybody knows that an 1197-pound man can't live on nothing. He now and again has to bring in a dozen hamburgers and a handful of Twinkies just to get through the morning.

I'm a bit like Walter Hudson: some days I have to bring in some hamburgers and Twinkies, not literal ones, but hamburgers and Twinkies of meaning. For instance, you let me have a really good day—or, alternately, let me get real good and disappointed—and you will find me sitting down at the piano in my living room and playing one of those old Baptist songs that I learned as a boy. For a while, and by myself, I take in some of those old songs just like Walter Hudson stuffing in a box of sausages and a dozen Twinkies. I stop thinking about holding on to pictures and being held captive by a picture and supreme fictions and about GUNS and PINS and the like. For a while, I enter into an old song and know deep down it is a good song that is part of a good picture, and I had better play it because that day it is the only song I have. If I don't play, at least once and a while—if ever so lightly—in the meaning of that song, I figure I might be left with sprouts and tea.

To be sure, I cannot now play in the meaning of those old songs in the same uncritical way that I did before I read all those books. I can never again enter into the pictures embedded in those old songs with what the philosopher Paul Ricoeur calls "first naiveté," which is to say that they will never be to me what they were when I was a child. But one can sometimes affectively, and even cognitively, enter into the old pictures with what Ricoeur calls "second naiveté." It is a delicate matter, affectively and cognitively, to hold and to be held by a picture, knowing that it is a picture; to dwell in a supreme fiction, knowing that it is a fiction.

Sometimes I play in a sturdy tune like "Be Still, My Soul," which uses that majestic tune "Finlandia." This song—or picture or fiction—uplifts and expands and is as nourishing as a hamburger with all the trimmings. Sometimes I turn elegiac and modulate into "Abide with me, fast falls the eventide. . . . The shadows deepen, Lord, with me abide." My friend Harrison Kohler told me not long ago that he wants that song at his funeral. I can understand why. It calms and centers. It mediates one's mortality in a consoling way. My mother's favorite is a hymn that transcribes the Twenty-Third Psalm. It's called "Surely Goodness and Mercy Shall Follow Me All the Days of My Life." Now there is a picture that is hard to hold on to if there ever was one.

The one I like best starts out "Come, thou Fount of every blessing, tune my heart to sing thy grace." I like the melody, but it is the central image that holds one. That image is of an unnamed, unspecified and thus unlimited, fountain. Now there's something to ponder: the possibility that at the center of reality there lies a fountain overflowing with blessing or—dare I say it—with love. That fountain, if one is attentive, can tune one's very heart to sing, to praise. This is a song about the possibility of singing a song. It thus is self-reflective; it recoils onto itself. Here you are singing a song, in tune, you hope; and you ask that your heart—your deepest self? your soul?—be tuned so as to be able to sing *another* song, a song of praise deeper, or higher, or fuller than the song you are now able to sing.

But you can never sing the full song. You'll never altogether be in tune with it. It always remains partially beyond your singing. That song is unreachable because the reality after which one's heart yearns is ineffable, unspeakable. The best you can do in your living room—and only sometimes, when you really need it—is to sing a song that approaches, reflects, or intimates that song. What you are singing is your yearning for the full song.

Sometimes when I play those old songs, I feel a bit embarrassed. That's why I usually prefer to sing them alone. I am not sure a fellow who has read as many books as I have ought to allow himself to be pulled into old songs and old pictures. It's not a post-modern thing to do. To tell the truth, I have thought for a long time about giving them up for good. But some days, they taste like hamburgers and Twinkies must taste to a fellow who has been trying to live on sprouts and tea.

## The Importunate Giver

Out of the corner of my eye, I noticed the note moving from student to student down the side of the seminar table in the Religion Department of Syracuse University. Our renowned teacher, Professor Stanley Romaine Hopper, was holding forth, about what I have no idea. Since I was at the end of the line, I assumed the note must be for me. There was no one else to pass it to. Holding the note just below the edge of the table, I opened it and read, "How would you like to teach at Le Moyne next year? Zog."

Ed Zogby and I were doctoral students, he a Jesuit priest and I a confused fugitive from the Southern Baptists, both of us studying religion and literature. We had known each other a bit, but nothing to make me expect what happened that day.

I had no idea what Zogby was talking about in the note. I didn't know that Le Moyne College existed, much less that it was a Catholic, Jesuit school across town in Syracuse and that Zogby had just been named chair of the religious studies department. I wasn't even sure that an erstwhile Southern Baptist should be talking to a Jesuit priest. My ignorance on that and other subjects didn't prevent my meeting with the dean the following week and, in September, beginning to teach part-time at Le Moyne, my first real teaching job.

I didn't know Zogby well, but I knew him well enough to know that he had read the literary critic Kenneth Burke; so in the seminars Zog was always saying something about the importance of our seeing life, as he said, "dramatistically." I wasn't altogether sure what he was talking about, but looking back, I see that, when considered dramatistically, the passing of that note—rather, the moment that I read the words "How would you like to teach at Le Moyne next year?"—is a turning point, an axial moment in the drama that is my life. As do the plots of many dramas and operas, everything—or a good part of everything—in my story follows from that note.

Ted L. Estess

    Neither Zogby nor I knew all that was going on at the time. Zogby needed someone to cover some classes. I would be writing my dissertation and he thought I might have some time and might need the money. I did. Maybe it was a passing fancy for him, just a thought that struck him that day in class. He was, after all, an impulsive person. I was guarded, deliberative, careful. We were opposites, who, as things turned out, were attracted to each other.

    Zogby could have directed the note to Bradley, my bright friend fresh out of Boston University and Yale. Or for Harry Weintraub straight from NYU. Weintraub knew more than anyone else in the class about every possible subject excepting what Professor Hopper was talking about, which was the manifold interrelationships of religion, poetry, and the psyche.

    Now that I think about it, I don't remember that my name was on the note. Zogby may well have intended the note for Bradley or Weintraub. Maybe it was all a mistake. I only assumed the note was for me. The plots of lots of plays work that way: the wrong person gets the note. When I assumed that the note was intended for me, perhaps Zogby politely went along. When I made the mistake, he just decided then and there, on the spur of the moment, to let it go. "He'll do," maybe that's what Zogby thought. He couldn't, at least while Hopper was talking, whisper down the table, "No, Estess, the note is for Bradley." So perhaps the plot of my life has turned on a mistake. Is that possible?

    I'd rather think that Zogby had given it some thought. He didn't want to misstep on his first hire. After all, he was taking something of a chance hiring the first Protestant into a Jesuit religion department, the first person, in fact, who was not a priest. I was, as I later learned, to replace the famous priest Daniel Berrigan, who had left teaching to give all his time to trying to stop the war in Vietnam. And since Zogby is a priest, maybe he even meditated before inviting me to teach for him. That would be good.

    If I had not gotten that note from Zogby, I would never have come home from Le Moyne College one day with two overcoats. Zogby gave them to me. He tried to give me another one, but it was too small. Sybil asked me what I was going to do with two more overcoats: I already had one. I didn't have a good answer. Another day I came home with three

## Fishing Spirit Lake

pipes. Zogby had pressed them on me as well. In our dining room in Houston, Sybil and I have a brown, leather-covered decanter, made and embossed in Spain. It was sitting on the credenza in Zogby's office the day I first saw it. He said, "Take this."

"What is it?" I asked.

"It's a decanter, you idiot. Don't you know what a decanter is?" I didn't tell Zog that I had never decanted anything in my life. Never seen anyone else decant anything either.

"Yes, Zog," I said, "I know what a decanter is. But I didn't know that that is a decanter."

"Well, it's a decanter. And *take* it." Zogby not only saw things dramatistically, he, by way of an expressive voice and the extraordinary malleability of his face, made every encounter into a mini-drama, a little play.

Zogby was an imperious gift-giver. He was nothing like the householder in that story that Jesus told. In the story, this householder and his wife have been asleep for hours when this fellow comes and knocks on the door. He knocks loudly, persistently, again and again. He is importunate, irritatingly so. The householder asks his wife, "Who's that sonnafabitch that keeps knocking on the damn door?"

Those are not Jesus' exact words, but you get the idea. The man asks, "Who the hell does he think he-iz?" Finally, the untimely visitor's importunity pays off. The wife says, "Open the door and see what the jerk wants, wil-ya?"

Zogby was the reverse of that householder. He would rush out in the middle of the night without the visitor even so much as knocking at the door, and he would start tossing things out, weighing him down with pastrami and pumpernickel, corn beef and rye, hummus and pita, black olives and mustard, Swiss cheese, a couple bottles of wine and some baklava. "Here, take this." he would say to the fellow before he opens his mouth, "and this, and this." He would insist, importunately, he would insist.

"Pardon me, sir," the fellow finally has a chance to say. And looking up over the great pile of pumpernickel and wine and pastrami, he asks, "Pardon me sir, I don't mean to bother you so late at night, but could you tell me how to get to the train station?"

That's the way it was that day in Zogby's office when he stood holding the decanter in his hand and poked it toward me. As was his wont, he rose in mock indignation. Puffed up like a Lebanese rooster, his ample rotundity displaying greater rotundity still, Zogby continued without ceasing.

"*Doonnn't* be silly," he said, "*taaakkke* it. Here, *taaakkke* it." Zog would draw out those words "doonnn't" and "taaakke," achieving thereby what my southern tongue achieved naturally.

"No, Zog," I said, "you've given me too many things already. That decanter looks nice right there on your credenza. You keep it."

As I protested, Zogby ascended almost to a shout; and punctuating each phrase with a short chop of the hand, he said, "Listen, Estess. Don't be an asshole. Take this decanter. That's an order." And as though to find justification for the importunity of his giving, he declared, "Take it to Sybil. She'll like it."

"Where did you get that?" Sybil asked when I got home.

"Ed gave it to me today at school."

"He gave you three pipes last week and the week before he gave you two overcoats."

"Today he gave me this."

"What is it?"

"It's a decanter. Don't you know what a decanter is?"

Life often works this way: you expect one thing and get something else. I went to Stanley Hopper's seminar that day aiming to learn something about religion and literature, but got a note that redirected the course of my entire life.

Many dramas, especially interesting ones, work like that. You are led to think that the story is going to turn out one way, say, that James is really going to close the big deal, marry Elaine, and move to Rochester, but no, James' business goes bad and he ends up destitute and Elaine loses interest in him. He then supports himself by playing the mandolin in subway tunnels in Manhattan and is finally picked up by a club down on Bleecker Street, only to end up making records for Folkway Artists—not only making records, but making money and helping preserve Appalachian folk music as well.

Not all dramas turn out so nice. Sir Walter Raleigh, I recall, tended to see all our plays as tragedies, so he wrote: "God, who is the author of all our tragedies, hath written out for us and appointed us all the parts we are to play." But Sir Walter was tossed into the dungeon for a long time and finally was done in in the old Palace Yard at Westminster Palace, London. He would tend to see our plays as tragedies.

But Zogby saw life as a comedy, as part, if you will, of a divine comedy, and it was largely due to him that the five years that I taught at Le Moyne College were comedic as well. They were so, in large part, because of the gifts I received. To tell the truth, every day was a gift, talking with students about things I thought were important. Some years later, I got a letter from one of them. It took me back to a conversation I had had over twenty years before. I was sitting in my office at Le Moyne when this student appeared.

"Dr. Estess," he said, "could I talk with you a minute?" I reproached myself for having left my door open.

"Dr. Estess, excuse me, but I'm Jerry Edwards. I wonder if I could do an independent study course with you this semester. I want to study Eastern religions."

"I don't know, Jerry," I said. "I've got about all I can handle already." I didn't tell him that I didn't know all that much about Eastern religions and that I would be doing the extra teaching gratis.

"I'd be happy with any time you could give me, Dr. Estess." I tried to discourage him, but he was sincere. A nice kid.

Years later, I get a letter. Out of the blue, it arrived on my desk in Houston. Hadn't thought of Jerry Edwards in twenty years. It came as a surprise and a gift, the letter did. Cheered my day and helped me get through the week. Jerry said he was finishing his residency in internal medicine. Just wanted to tell me about it. Said that that reading course in Eastern religion was the most important course he took in four years in college. It set him on a path that he still follows. After college, he turned seriously Eastern, ate brown rice, did yoga, meditated half the time, shaved his head, and went to live in an ashram. As I read the letter, it occurred to me that if I had known he was going to go to all that trouble, I wouldn't have taught him that course.

After several years living and meditating in the woods, he decided to become a doctor, an alternative doctor of sorts. He would combine

Eastern therapies and meditative activities with Western interventionist techniques. Now he's a meditating Catholic M.D. healing people and helping to make the world a better place.

Jerry Edwards wrote all that to me in the letter. Said he wanted to thank me for what I did for him. Said he was also working as a volunteer in a clinic for poor people. Wished me God's blessings and said that he hoped to see me if ever I get to Syracuse. I wrote him back, but haven't heard from him since. Perhaps I never will.

That's the way it is with much that we do in life, certainly with teaching. You get up every day and do what you do, putting life and soul into it. You're on stage, playing your part, and hoping to play it well. You get immediate gratification just from the performance of it. In the case of a teacher, some students respond and perhaps learn a few things.

Then that class, that task, that job, is over and you say, "I've had a good run," and you move on to the next act. Then twenty years later, if you are lucky, you get a letter thanking you. You are glad to get it. It brings something back you thought you had lost and makes you think that what you did counted for something.

But if a teacher is trying to give something, the student must receive. Some don't, or can't.

Ed Zogby ran into this problem more than once. One year Zogby was spending the holidays in Utica with his family. When he got up on Christmas day, he decided to drive the fifty miles back to Syracuse to visit the Jesuits who had remained at Le Moyne. They were older and without family and he would cheer them up.

So Zogby left his family in Utica and drove in a snow shower across the frozen hills of Upstate New York to Syracuse and found his way to the Jesuit residence on the college campus. Walking down the hallways, knocking on doors, hailing fellow priests on Christmas day, he was pleased with himself, a regular Tiny Tim bringing joy, turning chill to warmth, loneliness to fellowship.

Rounding the corner, Zogby saw Father Frank Fingerhut, the treasurer of the college, coming his way. Another opportunity to bring much needed good cheer.

"Frank," he told me that he had said, "it's good to see you, Frank. How *aarrrre* you, Frank?" Father Fingerhut was getting on in years, so

Zogby spoke loudly, and his voice rattled down the corridor, all the way to the president's suite. Father Reilly stuck his head out to see who was making all the noise. Zogby cringed at disturbing the president of the college on Christmas day.

"Hello, Eddie," Father Fingerhut said. "Is that you, Eddie?" Father Fingerhut's eyes were failing a bit; and in the shadows of the hallway, he had trouble making things out.

"Yes, Frank, it's me, Ed Zogby. How *aarrre* you, Frank? How *aarre* you?"

"I'm fine, Eddie, I'm doing just fine. As far as I know, Eddie, I'm doing fine, just fine."

"Frank, I drove over from Utica to wish you a Merry Christmas."

"What's that, Eddie? You drove over from Utica?"

"That's right, Frank. I drove over from Utica."

"Eddie, what were you doing in Utica? It's bad weather out there, you know, Eddie."

"I went over there to spend Christmas with my sister and her family. They live in Utica, Frank."

"Oh, I see, Eddie, I see." Zog told me that he had intended to talk with Fingerhut for a few minutes, but it seemed as if the conversation, such as it was, would never end.

"What are you doing here, Eddie? I thought you were in Utica with your family. But, Eddie, why did you come all the way over here from Utica?"

"I came over here, Frank, to wish you a Merry Christmas." And puffing himself up again like a grand Lebanese rooster, Father Edward Zogby, S. J., leaned up on his toes and crowed, "So, Merry Christmas, Frank. *Merrrrry, Merrrry* Christmas."

"Why, Eddie," Father Fingerhut said, "you ought not to have done *thaattt*."

Zogby came back to the office from the holidays still hyperventilating over Fingerhut's reply. He told me, "Estess, I tell you what I should have said. I should have said, 'Listen, Fingerhut, you asshole, I didn't come over here in a snowstorm from Utica because I ought to. I came over here, dammit, to wish you a Merry Christmas. The least you could do is say thank you.'" And raising his voice even further, Zogby repeated, "The least you could do is say thank you. *Asshole.*"

That's the way it sometimes goes for gift-givers, especially for impulsive, importunate ones. Sometimes they have things they can't give away, things that others won't or can't receive.

"What size shoe do you wear?" I was standing just inside Zogby's office. It was a spring day in Syracuse, and after six months of snow, sprigs of green were finally breaking through.

"Pardon?" I said.

"What size shoe do you wear?"

"Nine-and-a-half."

"Really? Nine-and-a-half?" Zogby got up from behind his desk and came to the side and bent over. With one hand on the desk for balance, he pulled the lace on one of his shoes. Slipping it off, he said, "Here, try this on."

"Ed, what are you doing?" By this time he had both shoes in his hand and was standing in his sock feet.

"Try these on. I think they'll fit."

"For God's sake, Ed, I'm not going to take your shoes."

"Here, just try them on. Don't you like these shoes?"

"They are nice looking shoes, Ed. That's not the point."

"Well, try them on. You'll like them."

"Ed, dammit, I'm not going to let you walk out of here in sock feet."

"It wouldn't matter. No one would notice."

"Ed, that's crazy. You keep those shoes. Besides, I wear a four-E. My football coach always said, 'Estess, other than an elephant you're the only thing in captivity that makes a round track.'"

"Did he really say that? That's funny."

"Yeah, that's what he always said. Because I wear a four-E." With that, I thought that I had deterred Zog in his importunity.

"These are wide shoes," he said. "Made off a wide last. Just try them on."

"They won't fit me, Ed. I can see. They won't fit me."

"They'll stretch. You wear them a few days, they'll stretch. It's good leather. See here." As though he were selling not giving, Zogby bent one of the shoes double and put his thumbs in the sides and stretched the leather.

"Ed, I'm not going to take your shoes. Thank you, I've got to go."

I escaped down the hall, passing our colleague Al Hennelly before reaching my office, Room 222. Zogby appeared at my door. I looked up to see him in his sock feet, shoes in hand.

"Here, try them on. If they don't fit, forget it. Just try them on."

"Ed, get out of here, please? I am not going to take your damn shoes."

Father Zogby turned and walked, sock feet and all, back to his office. I went to the door and watched him go down the hall, the shoes held together in his right hand. He looked like Charlie Chaplin lost on a deserted street, growing smaller and smaller the further he went. All he needed was a cane and bowler hat. Our colleague Al Hennelly looked out his door to see him walk by. Al chuckled. He couldn't imagine what Zog could be doing walking down the hall in his socks. Al looked to me. I shrugged.

I felt bad.

I still do.

At least I could have tried them on.

Fishing Spirit Lake

## Montana State of Mind

"Don't listen to this man." I shouted from the back of the lecture hall. Adams stood at the front, looking perplexed and irritated. Walking down the aisle, I exhorted the students, "Don't believe a word of it. Professor Adams is a dangerous man."

With my interruption, Adams puffed himself up and replied, "But ... but ... Professor Estess, I wouldn't have expected you to understand. But these excellent students, they know exactly what I'm talking about."

Adams and I played like that all year long, never being altogether serious or frivolous, all the time trying out things that we would be too timid to say elsewhere. Both of us were visiting professors at the University of Montana. We could fool around. We felt no compunction to be right. After all, what does it matter if you're wrong in Montana?

In October, the chairman of the art department mounted a faculty show and invited all faculty members to submit a piece of art. A would-be Marcel Duchamp hung a toilet seat on the museum wall. Another tacked up a trout. Someone posted a partial page from *Moby Dick*. The chairman wanted to take the show to Helena and mount it in the rotunda of the state capitol. That kind of thing happens in Montana. Why not? Really, who gives a damn what people imagine—or do—in Montana?

Most of us think that what we are about holds at least a tenuous relation with what goes on elsewhere. We imagine, or hope, that what we do makes a difference in the world. That's one of the little fictions that get us up in the morning and helps us through the day. By "fiction," I don't mean that this idea is necessarily false. I simply mean what the etymology of the word "fiction" suggests, which is that a fiction is something that human beings make.

True Montanans don't need that fiction. It's part of the Montana state of mind. Some boosters talk about making the economy of Montana productive and opening up avenues for international trade, but that's balderdash. Everyone knows that the reason you go to Montana is to be in Montana.

Once there, you can play around, fiddle with ideas, imagine possibilities, do things just for the hell of it. That's one reason poets and writers love Montana. In Montana, they can make up secondary worlds and imagine realities disconnected with what people take to be the real world elsewhere.

That's also why rich folks like Ted Turner and Tom Brokaw and Phil Jackson and a host of others flock to Montana and buy up all of it they can. Rich folks get tired of making money. They want to do something that doesn't amount to anything for a while, just for the hell of it. Being no count in Montana, that's what they're after. In that regard at least, rich folks and poets and true Montanans are a lot a like: they play.

That's why a man like Jacob Johns could never be content in Montana. Now it's true that Johns likely couldn't be altogether content anywhere, but it was certain he was going to be discontent when he left the faculty at a major university in the East and moved to Montana in the late 1960s. And since he was discontent, he figured he should do whatever he could to make everybody around him discontent as well.

As chairman and a reigning intellectual presence at the University of Montana, Johns presided over a department of midgets. In fact, he suffered an entire university of midgets. One giant among 9,000 midgets, that's how Johns saw things.

"I've done what I can to help Jeff," Jacob told me one evening as we lingered behind after everyone else had left for the day. "I brought him out here to help me, but he will never do any first rate work." As though suggesting that I might be an exception, Jacob proceeded to assess every member of his department, all of whom he had hired.

"Take Gardner," he said. "Gardner is trying to get by on what he did fifteen years ago. He wrote one book, college kids like it, but what do college kids know? And Morgan, well, Morgan drinks, plays golf, and chases women. I thought when I hired him he was going to do something, but he hasn't produced. He got those two books out, but they're marginal. And Geldner, we didn't give him tenure. The rest of the department wanted to keep him, but I told them that Geldner never will amount to much. You know what I told my colleagues, Estess? I told them that mediocrity breeds mediocrity. That's as clear as a goat's butt going uphill. You let one weak person slip by and pretty soon you've got no standards at all. This half-assed university never has had the courage to have any standards. That's why some of my colleagues wanted to let Geldner slip by. They're cowards."

As Johns started in on the president and dean and other university officials, I knew I would be no exception: I couldn't possibly measure up to this man.

In those days, before he was lucky enough to have a good heart attack, Jacob Johns made Faust look like Saint Francis. He was eternally striving. His reach always exceeded his grasp. He wanted to know everything about his field and expected people who worked for him to know as much or more about theirs. Ahab chasing Moby Dick, that's what he was.

One day, Johns said to me, "Estess, you've got to learn to live with infinity." Being a compliant young assistant professor, a visiting one at that, I nodded as though I knew what Johns was talking about. He didn't wait for a stupid reply from me.

"I do several things, Estess," he said. "Each one makes infinite demands on me. That's what you've got to learn: how to deal with infinity."

I didn't know what Johns was talking about, but I thought it was likely that he thought I should be working harder, producing more, getting on with my career at a faster pace. Johns didn't mention family or friends or horsing around. Those take a fair amount of time and energy as well.

Oddly, Jacob Johns could charm the socks off a rattlesnake, and if charm didn't get them off, he took to yelling. For charming and yelling, he beats any man I've ever known. He's the only man I know who helps me understand General Patton.

This became clear to me over Labor Day weekend of 1975. We had just arrived in Missoula when Johns invited Sybil and me and Jim and Robin Duke up to his cabin in the North Country. Jim was also a visitor in the department for a year. We drove out of Missoula toward Canada on Friday afternoon, turned west at the southern entry to Glacier National

Park, and headed up to Pole Bridge and continued north on the gravel road to Jacob's place, which sat on a creek that feeds into the North Fork of the Flathead River.

Johns charmed us all afternoon, and at night he gathered us around the wood stove, popped popcorn, and regaled us with stories from a half dozen universities in this country and Europe. He talked about everybody in five languages in his area of scholarship and told us how wrong they were. He even put us to bed.

"Sybil and Ted," he said, "it's going to get down to about twenty-five degrees and your cabin doesn't have any heat. We'll take some of those big rocks outside the door, put them in the fire here, and get them real hot. Then we'll wrap them in some towels and put them in a gunnysack. Put that sack in your sleeping bag and those rocks will stay hot all night."

Sybil and I woke the next morning and looked out to see a sprinkling of snow, right where a dozen deer had grazed the night before. The rocks were still warm in the sack.

In the afternoon General Patton went into action, only this time he wasn't moving five thousand tanks across Germany, he was moving Estess and Duke up the creek. I had made the mistake of telling Johns I wanted to catch some fish. Maniac that Johns is, he was not content to walk fifty feet from the cabin down to the river, stand on the sand bar, and see if we could land a few. He had to tear up the stream, right up the side of the mountain.

At lunch, Johns said, "These greenhorns come out here with all their fancy boots and gear, and they don't know any more about catching fish than I know about brain surgery. Estess, you got some old shoes?" I felt like a private in Patton's army, lifting my boot to let the General inspect my gear.

"Those will do," Johns said. I was relieved. "Estess, Duke," he said, "to catch fish you got to get in the water and move up the stream. When you get to a pool, cast in three or four times. You don't get a fish, you move on. You got to keep moving, you understand?"

Now I was an infantry officer before the final push against impenetrable lines. "Damn right, you old bastard, I can do it." That's what I wanted to say. "I'll get in the water. I'll keep moving. I'll find those goddamn fish. I'll show you, you old bastard."

# Fishing Spirit Lake

"It's not like it used to be up here," Johns said. "When I came up here twenty years ago, we would catch two, three hundred trout a morning, pull them out as fast as the fly hit the water. Then we would smoke 'em. Ever eat smoked trout, Estess?"

Before I had a chance to answer, he continued. "Things have changed. A lot of folks come out here and think you can catch fish just by dropping a fly in the water. They don't know you've got to get wet. When they find out, they won't do it. That's why they give up fishing. Too lazy."

In the afternoon we three men left the women in the cabin and piled into Johns' 1958 green panel truck, which he had salvaged from the Forest Service for a hundred bucks. He tore up the side of the mountain and along timber roads like a crazy man. If the road didn't go through, Johns went through anyway. If a log crossed the road, he went over. Jim Duke, who stood in at about five-feet-five and a hundred and forty pounds, was in the back seat. Duke started out as he always did, smoking his pipe. But we hadn't gone a quarter of a mile up the mountain, before Duke was coughing and sputtering. I didn't see that pipe again for the rest of the day.

"I need some shocks on this damn truck," Johns yelled as we banged into a washout on the road. "The springs are gone too." I nodded and looked around to see Duke's face as lemon-green as Johns' truck.

"This'll do," Johns announced, and he was out and ten yards toward the creek before I got the door open. "Follow me," he shouted over his shoulder. "I'll show you how to do it."

It was a humbling sight. Here was an internationally renowned scholar, a man of means and sometimes of manners, attacking that stream as though his life hung in the balance. Johns plunged into the water, hurtling logs and rocks, stopping for a minute or two to cast into a pool, only to say, "Got to keep moving. Come on, Estess, there's nothing in that pool. Step across that log, Duke. Get in the goddamn water, Estess."

He plunged far ahead, not looking back to see if Duke and I were keeping up. Duke's legs were mangled from falling against rocks and logs. His hands were raw from grabbing limbs and pulling himself through. He seemed to be at the brink of cardiac arrest. A full-time pipe smoker has no business being a part-time fishing partner of Jacob Johns.

Now and again Duke and I caught a glimpse of silver hair up above, just a glint in the light filtering through the trees. "Got one," we heard, and before we huffed up to see the prize, Johns was gone on up the stream, crashing, hurtling, plunging ahead, always up and ahead. "Got one." echoed down the slope. Duke and I abandoned all hope of fishing. It was all we could do to stay within range. Why we tried, I'll never know. I suppose we were afraid Johns would forget we were along and leave us on the mountain for the night.

Struggling to keep up, I imagined how our adventure might turn out. There Johns would be late in the afternoon, driving up to the cabin in his green Forest Service panel truck. "Hey, Sybil, Robin," he would yell. "Get out here." He stands there, alone by the truck with his string of fish. "I told you I would get some fish," he says. "They're beauties, aren't they?"

Diminutive Robin, she of soft voice and gentle face, screws up her courage to ask, "Jacob, where is Jim? And where is Ted?"

"Jim? Ted?" he asks, startled, astonished. "Did they go fishing?"

"Yes, Jacob," Robin says.

"Did they catch any fish?"

"We don't know, Jacob. We don't know where they are."

"I bring those men up here to the woods and they get themselves lost," Jacob shouts. "What do they expect, for God's sake? Somebody to hold their goddamn hand? Where did they go?"

"They left five hours ago with you, Jacob," Robin replies, her voice quivering as the shadows lengthen across the mountains.

"They left with me?" Jacob shouts, startled, astonished. "What the hell happened to them?"

"I don't know, Jacob. Don't you know?"

"Those men had better get their butts back to this cabin before the sun goes down. It's damn cold in these mountains at night."

"Jacob, don't you think we need to look for them? Try to find them? They, they might be lost."

"Robin, let me tell you one thing. If your half-assed husband comes up here and gets himself lost in these mountains, he'll have to find his own way out. There's not much you can do to help him, not tonight anyway. He—and what's that other fellow's name? Ted? If they go off fishing and get their butts lost, they'll have to find their own way home."

Now, tell me, how can a man like Jacob Johns be content in Montana? A man as driven, as determined to produce, as crazed with the need to make a difference in the world, that kind of man has no business being in the state of Montana. He should be given a visa to visit for a few days, something like the permit you get to camp in a wilderness area, but never allowed to move there. It is not good for him or for Montana.

A person who goes to Montana must be ready not to produce, not to make a difference. Unless you are a poet, whose business it is not to make a difference in the world, or unless you are rich or have a little extra money and want to play around, Montana is not for you.

That's why the country needs a place like Montana. If we didn't have Montana, we would have to create it, and we need it now more than ever. That's why I'm for saving all those wilderness areas out there. Montana probably has six billion acres of wilderness the purpose of which is to do nothing but be wilderness. It's against the law to do anything in the wilderness. We need places where it's against the law to do anything, where you've got to do nothing. We shouldn't let poets and rich folks get away with doing all the nothing. The rest of us should get in on it as much as possible, do as much nothing as we can get away with.

Now this state of mind frustrates the Jacob Johns of the world. They're afraid that people who are doing nothing are getting away with something. That's why Johns drove everybody out of his department there in Missoula. Those he didn't run off left if they could.

So it didn't surprise me that ten years later, weary of living among 9,000 midgets and disgusted with being discontent, Johns just left Montana, even sold his cabin on the North Forth, said he didn't intend to go back and didn't want his kids to either.

These days, just looking at Montana, you would never know Jacob Johns was ever there. Now he's out in Sonoma where everybody is working their butts off to bottle one more bottle of wine. They're so busy producing wine, they hardly have time to drink the stuff.

All this goes to show that one man can't change Montana. Johns wanted to make Montana a sweatshop and turn Montanans into Yankee beavers. Here Montanans would be, busy beavers, all 900,000 of them, sweating from morning till night, *chomp, chomp, chomping*, cutting down all those trees, pulling them up the rivers and across the ponds and lakes, building all those dams and rearranging all that wilderness, *chomp, chomp, chomping*, determined to take down 610 billion trees as fast as possible, Yankee beavers all.

Johns would be happier in Japan where everybody is a beaver. Now that I think about it, maybe that's why Johns left Montana: it isn't Japan.

I sometimes wonder how things would have been if I had taken that job that Johns offered me and if Sybil and I had stayed in Montana. I don't know, but I suspect that, despite Johns, I would have gotten better at doing nothing. You can't stay around people who are doing nothing a lot of the time without some of it rubbing off on you. Maybe I would have warmed up to the possibility that whatever I do might not finally make a great deal of difference in the world. My dancing friends Bessie Snyder and Bill Bevis would have seen to that.

I had to go all the way to Montana to learn to dance. Here I was at about the age when the great poet found himself lost in the woods and I had never really learned to dance. Maybe the poet got lost in the woods because he didn't dance.

The Baptists pretty well did me in for dancing. Because of them, I gave it and a lot of other things up without ever doing them. They told me dancing would lead to other things. When I was a young man, I tried dancing a few times and decided the Baptists are right: it does lead to other things.

It was strange, then, to meet Doug Adams in Montana and to learn that he specializes in religion *and* dance. That was almost as strange as my reading a little book by a philosopher named Sam Keen called *To a Dancing God*. Before, they never seemed to go together, religion and God and dance. I had not yet read Nietzsche where he writes, "Never worship a god who doesn't dance."

Bessie Snyder was my dance teacher in Montana. She was a dancing Virgil to my droopy Dante. Bessie lived with a dog named Benjy in an A-frame next to our house on Rattlesnake Creek. Benjy's gray and white hair was so long you couldn't see his eyes, but he got around better than any long-haired, three-legged English sheep dog I've ever known. Having only three legs made Benjy a little skittish, and he wanted to be with Bessie all the time. I couldn't blame him for that. The first time that Benjy relaxed with me was when I went over to his house to watch the sixth game of the '75 Series on Bessie's TV. Had I not been in Montana I would not, I'm almost sure, have given up my books for baseball. If so, I would have missed what many people consider the greatest World Series game of all time. That's when Carlton Fisk hit that home run against the Reds and won the game in Fenway Park. Fisk danced up the first base line after hitting the ball, waving both arms, sympathetically trying to keep the ball fair. He was carrying on like he had done something when, if truth be told, he was celebrating the glorious feeling of having done nothing gloriously.

Bessie Snyder's dance class met on Thursdays, and she signed Sybil and me up. Benjy went along to watch. There I was, one of a few men and the oldest by far, in red sweat pants on the hardwood floor of the student union building at the University of Montana. The twenty women, all in leotards, were agile and slim. I was stiff and, as my mother used to say, "husky."

"Here we go," pert and petit Bessie said, and the jazz tape started, and we moved to the left and then to the right. "Lift those legs and clap those hands. Sixteen right and sixteen left. Back we go, all the way back."

I felt like a long-haired, three-legged sheep dog on a hardwood floor. I couldn't get my leg up in the right time. I enjoyed Bessie's bobbed hair and dancer's body, but mine wouldn't move with the beat. It had no rhythm.

One Thursday night, Bessie shouted above the music, "You're doing great, Ted. That's great." Something had happened. It wasn't fascinating, but I had rhythm. Benjy tapped his nub, and I raised my leg with the ease of a dog pissing on a fire hydrant. By late November our house on the Rattlesnake turned into a honky tonk, a regular road house on the Rattlesnake. People came there just to boogie. Two other professors at the university, Bill Bevis and his wife Juliet were the Montana Astaire and Rogers and they led the group. I envied Bill dancing with his two beautiful step-daughters, nine-year-old Mary Catherine and five-year old Sarah. All of them were there, religion, God and dance, whooping it up.

But I finally decided it wouldn't be good for me to live full-time in Montana. I never would get use to the tension between Jacob Johns and Montana. That tension—between beating everybody else and doing nothing—would be too much for me, just like it was for Russell Morgan. That's why Morgan drank and chased women, why his afternoons were too long. He couldn't figure out whether he should be beating everybody else or doing nothing. Johns told Morgan to beat everybody else. Montana told him to do nothing. So he tried to beat everybody in the morning and do nothing in the afternoon and night. He did neither with a clear conscience. Maybe that's why, late one night in August of 1982, he took off his clothes, went out to his garage, crawled into his Suburu, and started the engine. The paperboy found him the next morning.

As my year in Montana wore on, the tension got to me. My eyes began to follow longingly after every young woman who crossed my path. It took more bourbon to warm the night. Sybil tied me to the mast to get me through. A famous Montana poet trying to deal with alcohol told me one afternoon, "You know the problem with being sober? What to do with all that time." I began to understand what he was talking about.

Late in May of 1976, several of us in the department went over to Eugene, Oregon, for the last professional meeting of the academic year. Sybil and I drove over early to visit our friends Carolyn and Martin Winch and their two kids in Bend, just east of the Cascades and about sixty miles east of Eugene. I've always thought that that family knows how to manage the tension: out there in the desert, they can do nothing without thinking they're wasting time; they can do something without trying to beat everybody else.

On Saturday morning, I left for the meeting, driving across the sandy flats and up through the mountains, then dropping down to the Willamette River valley to Eugene, not far from the ocean. Martin had told me that I had to see the rhododendrons, which in late May are in full bloom in Eugene. At the meeting, I listened to one guy read his paper and decided to take a break and go visit the rhododendrons before lunch.

The closest thing in my experience to rhododendrons were azaleas in Mississippi. But azaleas don't measure up to rhododendrons. I had never seen such profusion of blossom, such extravagance and tomfoolery of color and delicacy of petal as I did that morning in Eugene. Blossoms billowed, reminding me of great piles of cotton that I saw as a boy, only these rhododendron piles were decked out in soft pastels, some in colors I could not name.

Back at the meeting and sitting down to another paper, I found it was too much. I couldn't hold in tension a rhododendron garden and a professional meeting. I leaned over to Morgan and said, "Sorry to miss your paper. I'm leaving. I'll read it back in Missoula."

Morgan whispered, "What's up, Estess? You find some action somewhere?"

I stopped to see the rhododendrons again, and then left town. I didn't know the best way, but figured any road heading west was going there. Thirty miles out, I stopped at a country store to ask directions. "Yep," the man at the counter said, "go as far as you can that-away and you'll run right into her. Can't miss her." I paid him for a bottle of champagne and two boxes of animal crackers.

The man in the store was right: I couldn't miss her. In fact, I smelled her five miles away. I lowered the windows in the car and bathed in her airs. Just over the next rise, there she was, resplendent in the early afternoon light. The wind whisked across her, stirred her up, and chased her away. She came back, again and again, as though she couldn't leave me, and just in time for me to step in. I wanted to dance with her all afternoon, barefoot in reality.

I lay down beside her, opened the bottle of champagne and drank straight from the bottle and gave her a toast. She drew away, but came back. The animal crackers tasted good, a tiger, a hippopotamus, and especially a giraffe. I gave her one of each, something like an offering, I suppose. She took them away and came back for more and more.

I lay down beside her and napped for a while. I hated to leave her, but it was time. The afternoon was too short.

"What are you doing here?" my friend Martin exclaimed as I appeared at his door in the desert. It was after ten and very dark. "You are supposed to be at that meeting in Eugene."

"I couldn't do it," I said. "I mean, I didn't want to do it, to stay at the meeting. I checked out at noon."

I didn't tell him, because I didn't know, all of the story. I told only the part I knew, how I went to the meeting and took a rhododendron break, and then checked out of the motel and headed west and bought champagne and animal crackers, how I lay down beside her, took a nap, and made love to my life.

Fishing Spirit Lake

## The Day I Flew in a Canoe

All year long, I enjoyed saying, "I live up the Rattlesnake." Others would say, "I live down the Bitterroot," or "out the Blackfoot," or "on the Clark Fork." People in Missoula, Montana, know each other by the rivers and creeks that measure the space of their lives in the valley.

But the Rattlesnake was our companion all through our year there. Sybil and I loved it. The sound of the water crossing the stones changed from month to month, really from day to day, and within a single day. We arrived after the drought of the summer. The water rustled moderately across the gray and orange, white and reddish stones. Ouzels stood on one leg and dipped their beaks quickly in and out of the creek. We waded in, scared off the ouzels, and gathered five stones. In Houston, these stones lie in our living room, silent reminders of the crisp water of the Rattlesnake.

In winter, it was *diminuendo*. Ice hung to the rocks and snow covered the ice. With the spring thaw in late May and June, the sound nearly overcame the house and us. One morning I woke and thought the water was over the banks and coming in. We closed our bedroom window against the sound, just to get some sleep. I told Sybil that I would never live next to another creek. About that time, students from the university came by the window, tubing the Rattlesnake. I envied them their fun. They laughed hysterically and held onto the inner tubes that carried them down the Rattlesnake and into the Clark Fork, a mile or so below us. One youngster fell off his tube just above our house. They found his body later that day. The newspaper said he crashed his head against the stones.

Early that fall of 1975, we got out to other creeks and rivers. I don't know how it happened, but Sybil and I made friends with Bob Hausman and Bill Bevis and their wives. By the end of September, Bob and Bill had us on the Bitterroot. I was with Bob in his raft, while Bill darted about in his wooden canoe, an antique beauty that he rescued from an old guy in

New Hampshire. In the raft, Bob and I moved steadily in one direction, downstream. Bevis glided up and down and across. He did circles around the raft, pirouettes in the water. Bob and I lumbered on.

Bevis is a master player and a lover of poetry. He climbs mountains with a woman and gets stuck on the side of Mont Blanc for three days in a snowstorm and barely survives a nosebleed. He catches fish when others do not, and flies into the wilderness in Alaska and crash lands, jumping out of the plane only to say, "I knew that would come to a bad end." He backpacks in the wilderness, doing everything outdoors with consummate grace and beauty. He laughs a lot and makes others laugh. He out-dances Sammy Davis and joins a Black Baptist Church choir in North Carolina and sings a jazzy "Just a Closer Walk with Thee." He's the best storyteller in western Montana, and wears crazy clothes, such as that white linen suit with straw hat and green tennis shoes that he wore to the Derby Day party Sybil and I gave alongside the Rattlesnake. We drank mint juleps. Late in the afternoon everyone stopped to watch Bill and his wife Juliette dance. Juliette teaches dance at the university, and she and Bill are a Montana Astaire and Rogers, or so they seemed that May Day in Missoula in 1976. You cannot but envy Bill Bevis.

Bob Hausman and I did as we lumbered down the Bitterroot in the stodgy, gray rubber raft that Bob sometimes uses to take greenhorns from back East in search of good trout fishing. Bob is like me, an endomorph lowlander, stocky and grown paunchy. He's lost two wives and about two thousands pounds in the last twenty years. He grew up poor and knows that dollars are hard to come by, and he spends the best part of the fall in Montana hunting elk and deer.

"Look at that Bevis," Bob said of his friend, "just look at him handle that canoe. Damn show-off. But it's beautiful. Before I forget it, Ted, don't ever get in a canoe with Bill Bevis. You've got to know what you're doing in these rivers before you try them in a canoe."

"Hey, Ted," Bob continued, turning his eyes from Bevis. "Look at that Tweedy bird." A bird, species unrecognizable to me, skimmed across the Bitterroot in the distance, barely visible to my eyes.

We floated on down the river, whiling away the time. "Hey, Ted," Bob said again, "Look there. There's another Tweedy bird."

This second bird was clearly different from the first, even to my lazy eyes, but I didn't say anything. I didn't want him to think that I didn't know what he was talking about. I didn't want to seem a greenhorn.

"Hey, Ted, I be damn. There's another Tweedy bird."

"Hausman, what the hell are you talking about? You've called three birds Tweedy birds, and each is different from the others. What are you talking about?"

"Ted, in Montana we call any bird a Tweedy bird that's not a duck." Bob's hearty chuckle drifted across the cool waters of the Bitterroot, and I knew that I had found a friend.

"Estess," Bill began to say to me along about February, "I want you to ride the river with me when the spring thaw comes. You've got to do that before you leave Montana." In his high pitched, nasal voice, Bevis vowed, "You'll love it, Ted. It's great, really great." And he laughed.

Back then Bevis was an evangelist for experience. Experience as such was a good thing. To him, it was clear: Estess hadn't ridden in a canoe in spring runoff in Montana, therefore Estess needed to ride in a canoe in spring runoff. Estess would love it, if for no other reason than that Estess hadn't done it. Isn't that always the case? You love doing what you haven't done before?

The phone rang on our last Sunday morning in Missoula. It was the twelfth of June and the Rattlesnake crashed outside our window. The water was cloudy, even muddy. "It's Bill," Sybil said as she called me to the phone. "He wants to take you on the Clark Fork this afternoon." She walked behind me as I went to the hallway, speaking to my back. "You can't go. It's too dangerous, Ted. Ted, you don't know anything about canoes. You remember that student who died in the Rattlesnake three weeks ago. Ted, you can't go in that canoe with Bill Bevis."

"Hey there, Bill. How are you. This afternoon? That's great, Bill, that'll be great, about two."

"Ted, I told you that I won't let you ride in a canoe in that river. Have you looked at that water? Bill Bevis knows what he's doing in a canoe. You don't. You could listen to me once and a while."

Bill told Sybil to pick us up just below the bridge at four o'clock, and he and I headed up the Clark Fork with the canoe strapped on top of his car. He had brought his aluminum canoe. Said he didn't like to take the wooden one into the river when he couldn't see the rocks. And the aluminum was more stable, less likely to capsize.

"Now, Ted, here's what we're going to do. I'll be in the back of the canoe, and you'll be in the front on your knees. I'll do most of the paddling, but I'll tell you when I need you. If we should go over—and I don't see why we should—here's how we'll handle it."

I remembered what Hausman had told me when we were in the raft floating down the Bitterroot.

"First, Ted, we won't panic. People get in trouble if they panic. If we go over, hang on to the canoe. I'll be talking to you, but I'll want you to get hold of the rope that is tied to the front of the canoe. We'll have to get the canoe at an angle to the current. Once we get the canoe at an angle, the current will take us to the bank. Don't worry. I'll tell you what to do. Just tie that life jacket on tight. I don't want it coming up and choking you. We'll have a short ride, but it'll be great. Anybody who comes to Montana needs to ride the river in the runoff."

Sybil was to wait at the bridge like Bill told her to. Later she said that she just knew something had happened. Said she couldn't wait until four o'clock. So she left and drove up river to look for us. I don't know what she thought we would have done if we had gotten to the bridge and she wasn't there.

The last thing I remember Bill saying as I turned around to see what he wanted me to do was, "You're doing great, Ted. Isn't this great?" Bill's high-pitched nasal voice was smothered as we turned into the water.

We later estimated that we were in the canoe not more than ninety seconds. Sybil was right: this was dangerous, and it didn't take a safety engineer to figure it out. I did exactly what Bevis told me to do: I panicked. Actually, I was beyond panic. I was overtaken with complete terror, but I was completely in control. Bevis was right: this was unlike anything I had experienced before. I didn't think I was capable of it, that anyone was capable of it. I didn't know the experience could be experienced. I had known terror without control, and control without terror. But catapulting down the Clark Fork River on a Sunday afternoon in June, I experienced absolute terror and absolute control—simultaneously. Beyond panic, I had absolute confidence in myself, not because of myself, but because I had absolute confidence in Bill Bevis.

"Hey, Ted. You all right?" Bill's sharp voice served us well, because

I could hear him above the roar. I held onto the canoe and wondered if my heart were going to explode.

"I think so," I yelled back. We had been in only seconds, but we must have gone a hundred yards. The water was near muddy, and the sound was like turbines at a generating plant. My head bobbed up as the life jacket did its work, and I caught sight of pieces of wood and other debris, which, like me, were riding the rapids of the Clark Fork down toward the Blackfoot and Bitterroot.

"You got the rope?"

"No."

"Dive under and find it. It's hanging down from the tip of the canoe. You've got to get it." For a millisecond, I knew I wouldn't do it. I would not go under the water and the canoe and find the rope. I knew I could not. But in a millisecond, I knew I would. I was under the torrent, this time with eyes open. I held to the gunnel and stabbed for the rope. I thought that the rush of water might wash the eyes out of my head. Is that possible, for water to jerk one's eyes right out of the sockets? Later I dreamed it was.

"Get it?" he yelled. "That's great. Now, listen. You've got to swim toward the right bank. We're closer to the left, so we head that a way. You've got to go under the canoe to the other side. Okay?"

I didn't say a word, but it was not easier the second time under. I didn't want to do it. By this time, we must have traveled a half-mile down stream, and I thought I should be cold. Bill had said that the water temperature was probably about 35, maybe 38 degrees. "It was snow this morning," he had said as we stopped the car.

"Great." he said, as I came up on the other side of the canoe. "Ride 'em, Cowboy. We've got it made. Just hold on. Wow. This water is cold. You cold?"

I couldn't answer. The water was tearing us down stream, and I wanted out. I just wanted out.

"Now, hold onto the rope, and swim toward the right bank. I'll swim the other way." I knew every muscle would tear this time as I side-stroked toward the bank, my left hand on the rope and my right reaching out to pull against the water. My clothes pulled me downward, but I kicked.

"Hang on, Cowboy. Here we go." We both held our positions and the on the Clark Fork. You've heard how I experienced absolute terror and control at the same time. How I made it because my friend Bill told me to make it. How we flew in a canoe.

## We're Having a Baby

### I

"We did it!" Sybil exclaimed. "We're having a baby."

"Great. That's great." was all the response I could manage.

"I am at a maternity shop in Rice Village," she said. "I'll be home soon." For Sybil, there is no slip between the cup and the lip: she checks out the maternity clothes ten minutes after learning she is pregnant.

Turning out the light in my study, I put down my frayed copy of *The Last Gentleman* by Walker Percy and went downstairs to start supper. It being tax day, I counted the months to see if that kid might possibly give us a deduction for '79. But leave that for later. Tonight we would celebrate. After all, it was past due: Sybil and I were both thirty-seven and had been married thirteen years. That should be enough time for anybody to make a baby.

I gave my youth to books and teachers and to thinking about life; otherwise, Sybil and I might have gotten started earlier. I'd be a grandfather now, like my high school friends. They're playing golf. Sybil and I are trying to figure out how to pay college tuition.

But I have no regrets. Old enough to be my son's grandfather, I've been able to act like one. Older parents have more fun. They figure they won't be around long enough to suffer the damage their kids do, so what the hell, enjoy the kids and forget the consequences.

The phone rang again at about 6:45. The rain had been falling steadily and hard, and I had finished the best part of a bottle of wine. "Ted, it's awful," Sybil said. "When I left the maternity shop, I turned on to this street and the water was too high. Ted, the water came up into the car. I had to wade out. It was up to my waist."

"Are you are right?" I asked.

"I got soaked. I made it to the apartment of a Rice student, and she gave me some clothes to put on. I'm there now, but the car is flooded."

"Did you buy any maternity clothes at the shop?" I asked.

"Ted, I'm not interested in maternity clothes. I'm worried about the car. It's flooded, Ted."

"How did that happen?"

"I told you how it happened. Haven't you been listening to the news? Houston is flooded. Thousands of cars are stranded. This wouldn't have happened if you had gone to the doctor with me. Ted, why didn't you go to the doctor with me?"

Six weeks pregnant and I had already made my first mistake as a father. Maybe I wasn't cut out to be a father.

I almost wasn't. For millennia, until about 1968 or so, couples got together and made babies. They didn't think about doing it: they did it. But many in my generation weighed the options and calculated the costs. We were free to organize life and time as we wanted. It was said that women shouldn't be trapped or repressed by children. I was a good person in those days: I didn't want Sybil to be trapped or repressed, I really didn't.

Since then, I've learned that too much deliberation and calculation can freeze the life right out of you. Just a few weeks ago I read an article about a new organization for disappointed women. It is called "WOC—Women Without Children." These women are not disappointed for the usual reasons, but because they delayed too long, or almost too long, before trying to make babies. Tens of thousands of women in their late thirties and early forties are panicky, fearing it may be too late. Now they are organizing support groups and talking about how women without children can still be empowered.

Had it not been for a therapist named Michael, Sybil and I might have been in the same fix: too late. Early in 1979 we were sitting in Michael's office when I said, "Michael, Sybil and I are thinking about having a baby."

"How long have you been thinking about it?" he asked.

"Ten or eleven years."

Michael answered, "You two know you can't make babies by thinking about it, don't you?"

"Michael," Sybil said, "you can't imagine the pressure that's put on a woman to have a baby. My mother has been pestering me about it for years. I can't live my life without people asking me, 'When are you going to have a baby?' And I tell you something else, Michael, I can't stand to be around people who have a new baby. They act like they invented babies. It makes me sick."

"Well, Sybil," Michael said, "you have to remember that having babies is important to people. It's not as important as breathing, but it's pretty close. It's biology, understand me?"

"But Michael," I said, "that doesn't mean everybody has to have babies. You don't have any babies."

"Ted," Michael said, "I'm gay, remember?" He mercifully continued. "There is more than one way to live a life, but I think I would have enjoyed being a father had things been otherwise. It sounds like you two have made a problem out of something that could be a pleasure."

"But, Michael," Sybil said, "I wanted to finish my degree; and before that, Ted was in school and I didn't want to stay home and take care of any snotty-nosed baby."

I added, "And I wanted to get settled in my job, and now Sybil wants to. Both of us are trying to get some writing done."

"And Michael," Sybil interrupted, "having a baby is not like it used to be."

"To tell you the truth, Sybil, I wasn't aware that the plumbing had been changed."

"Michael, You know what I am talking about. You know that women can't be expected to do nothing but have babies. And I can't stand babies, all that poop and all those diapers."

"That's right," I announced. "Sybil and I want to be equal partners in whatever we do." Michael cackled, he roared.

"What's so damn funny?" I asked, shouting above Michael's hilarity.

"You two," he said, "listen to me. If you wait until you settle all these things, you'll never do much of anything in life. Stop thinking about it. Make a baby. You two will be fabulous parents. Go to it."

So we did. And Sybil ended up flooding out our brand new Mercury Cougar on April 15th, 1979.

## II

Ted L. Estess

Natural childbirth was the thing in those days, so Sybil and I signed up for the Lamaze class at Methodist Hospital. Along about the end of September, we were sitting on the floor with eight other expectant couples.

"Now, mothers, lie down," the trainer instructed, "and let's practice breathing. Fathers, you count." The room looked like a field of prairie dog mounds. Any second, I expected a little brown prairie dog to stick his nose out from behind one of those mounds and check the weather.

"That's great, you're doing great," the instructor said. I wondered what folks did before Lamaze as I said, "One, two, three," and Sybil inhaled and exhaled.

Sitting there, I remembered the Arab doctor who came to see Sybil in Jerusalem a month or so earlier. We were staying for a week in the American Colony Hotel, which is in East Jerusalem not far from what was called the Mandelbaum Gate before the '67 war. One night, Sybil became nauseated and the hotel called a doctor. He came at around 5 a.m.

We were in a grand room, spacious and airy. From out the window we could hear the muezzin singing the call to prayer from the minarets on the hills nearby. With fourteen-foot ceilings and 19th-century furnishings, the room smelled of strange spices and old secrets. Outside, the ancient city awakened to a new day.

In the shadows of the room, the Arab doctor prescribed medicine and said that it wouldn't hurt the baby and that Sybil would feel better later that day. We told him that Sybil had had amniocentesis and we already knew that the baby was a boy. He had no interest in amniocentesis and very little, for that matter, in Sybil's nausea. He was interested only *that* a baby was going to be born. It was as though he were a messenger, perhaps a wise man from an ancient eastern place, arriving in the early light to encourage and instruct us in the ways of birth. He spoke of women who squat in the field and deliver their babies and walk to the road and catch the next bus to their village, baby in arms. People on the bus always stand to let new mothers sit down. He said that modern life had cut birth off from life, from death too. Birth had been put in the hospital and people didn't see birth and death mixed in with daily work in the shops and fields and homes. Modern women weren't weaker: they had just learned new ways of thinking. Traditional women had much to teach if we would listen.

That's what the dark and quiet doctor told us in the shadows of early morning light in Jerusalem. I asked how much I owed for his visit. "No money, no money," he said, shaking his head. "I stopped by on my way to my office. It was no trouble. I didn't do anything. God's blessing on your wife," he said. "God's blessing on you and your baby."

The room in the Methodist Hospital was all light as the optimistic young Lamaze teacher instructed us on the techniques of natural childbirth. "Mothers and fathers," she insisted, "you must practice breathing together every day. And, mothers, next week I want each of you to bring a picture of a beautiful scene. It can be of a mountain stream or an ocean, anything. You have to be able to focus on your scene and breathe right."

I was determined to be a good Lamaze father. I would help Sybil breathe right and focus. With only four months to go, I was afraid we wouldn't have enough time to get it right. I told Sybil that we should have started a month or two earlier learning how to breathe. She said she wished we had too. I told her that we needed to practice more and that she needed to focus harder. She promised she would.

"Now before we leave," the instructor said, "I want every father to tell us what having a baby means to you. You fathers are having a baby, too, and I want each of you to tell us what has happened to you since you got pregnant."

An awkward silence filled the room. I looked over at Robert who looked around at Monaco who stared across at Charlie who glanced at David who seemed embarrassed as he looked at Duane who shifted his eyes to Eric who dropped his eyes into his lap and shifted his weight. There is no comfortable way for pregnant men to sit on the floor.

"Okay, Duane, you first, okay?" the instructor said, and I thought Duane was going into cardiac arrest.

Weakly, he replied, "Okay. Well," Duane said, "well . . . well, I don't know. It's just been great, you know. I mean Cheryl here has been great . . . I don't know . . . it's just been great." Duane looked like a drowning man. What else could he say? It was just great.

"That's wonderful, Duane, thank you very, very much," the instructor said.

"And Robert, what about you?" Robert was an air conditioning engineer at the hospital. Every week, he came to class in his gray overalls, and on the pocket, I could read in italicized red letters *The Methodist Hospital*. And beneath that, *Engineer*. Robert's wife Luann glowed, sitting there beside him.

All of a sudden, tears began streaming down the engineer's face. He struggled to find voice to say anything at all. Little Luann glowed ever brighter. I wondered if somebody had plugged her in.

Between sobs, Robert blurted such words as he could. "It's the most wonderful thing," he sobbed, "that has"—sob, sob—"ever . . . ever"—sob, sob—"ever happened to me." Luann beamed, triumphant.

The instructor mercifully moved on to Monaco.

"Well," Monaco said in a loud voice, "the worst thing that's happened is that she"—and he pointed a finger toward his wife Francine—"she got fat. She's gained about thirty pounds. She can't hardly git around. Just look at her. She can't walk from here to the goddamn door. I told her to quit eating all that junk, but she keeps on packing it in."

Visibly shaken by such insensitivity, the instructor called on Eric. "Honestly," Eric said softly, "it's just brought Amy and me a whole lot closer to the Lord. I tell Amy, 'The Lord did it, he did it all.' When we do our breathing exercise, I say, 'One, two, thank-you-Jesus, five, six, thank-you-Jesus.' That helps Amy relax, you know. I tell her the Lord is going to be right there with us in the delivery room, and we thank him for it, yes, Jesus, thank you, thank you, Jesus." Eric turned to Amy and they looked sweetly into each other's eyes. The rest of us were real happy for them, we really were.

When it came my turn, all the good stuff had about been said. So I added, "I'm like Francine: I can't get enough to eat. All hours of the night and day, I want to eat everything I can get my hands on. I've already gained twelve pounds, and we've got three months to go. I crave pickles, those big dill pickles. I can't get enough of those big things. Sybil's doing great, and I'm having a good time, but I just can't stop eating."

I know I was a disappointment to the Lamaze instructor. She thought I was being a smart-aleck. Better to cry like Duane or praise the Lord like Eric than be a smart-aleck college professor.

But Sybil cackled in laughter. In fact, during those pregnant months, I sometimes thought she had caught laughing sickness.

At Thanksgiving, my parents came over to Houston from Mississippi to visit us, and they made me feel better. My father told me not to worry too much about how I was doing in that course on natural childbirth. He said his mother had all eight of her babies in the bedroom on the farm in Mississippi. That's where he was born in 1912. Aunt Meletha was the midwife, and Dr. Brumfield stopped by a day or so later to see how things were going. My mother didn't know anything about her birth. She supposed it was at home in the big house in Simmonsville. Her mother never talked about it, she said. But my mother said that when I was born, the doctors kept her in the hospital for almost two weeks. It was the normal thing to do at the time. She said she was exhausted by the time she got home from that hospital.

"Sybil," my mother said, "I see the baby kicking." We were sitting in the den that Thanksgiving evening, barely able to breathe after so much cornbread dressing. My mother laughed. Sybil did too. "Ansel," she said to my father, "I told Sybil I see the baby kicking."

"LaVerne," Sybil announced, "that baby is kicking all the time now. I talk to him and try to quiet him down, but he just keeps on kicking. Did you talk to Ted before he was born?"

"Goodness, I don't remember if I did or not. I doubt it."

We went to bed that night, and I was glad that my parents were sleeping across the hall from Sybil and me. I knew that they were happy to be expectant grandparents. I felt good making them happy.

Going to sleep, I put my hand on Sybil's stomach and felt our baby kicking. "I think that boy wants to come outta there," I said.

"He's welcome to come on out whenever he wants to," Sybil said. "It'll be all right with me."

## III

After kicking for another month, Barrett Estess came out into the world on New Year's Day, 1980, in the Methodist Hospital in Houston, Texas, seven floors up from that well lighted room where Sybil and I went to the Lamaze classes. By 5:30 that afternoon, we had forgotten all that stuff, the breathing, the focusing, the techniques of childbirth. That's when Sybil was wheeled into the operating room for an emergency Cesarean. I was glad she was not squatting in a field in the Middle East or lying in a farmhouse in Mississippi attended by Aunt Meletha. I was glad Dr. Keith Reeves was in charge. He said he could deliver a baby by Cesarean in ninety-seconds if he had to. Standing in the operating room watching him, I saw no reason to doubt it. He said later that most likely Sybil would have died, and surely the baby, without the Cesarean.

We had left the house at about 5 that morning anticipating that things would go differently. We had almost everything we needed, just like we had learned in the Lamaze class. I had surprised the teacher and myself by becoming a well-trained, disciplined, and determined Lamaze father. Sybil's mother had sent some copies of *Reader's Digest* out from Mississippi for us to read in case there was a lull in the proceedings. She said we would enjoy those articles; they're short and we could finish them while we waited. Sybil had a cassette recorder with a tape of a flowing mountain stream to help her relax. I had a clock with a big second hand to time her breathing, along with a note pad to make some notes. I needed to be able to tell the nurse what was happening. The instructor had said that my feet would get real tired from my standing up all day, so I took along an extra pair of shoes like she told me to. We had two cameras in case one of them went bad and six rolls of film and extra batteries and some Life Savers to suck on if our mouths got dry. Sybil said her picture of the beautiful mountain stream would go well with the tape of the water flowing.

In the rush to leave home that morning, we forgot the two roast beef sandwiches the instructor said would keep me from fainting. She said I wouldn't have time to go down to the cafeteria and that the nurses didn't want another father to faint from hunger or dehydration. About three blocks from home, I realized that I had left the sandwiches on the kitchen counter. Sybil said it was important for us to have everything and that her labor pains were still twelve or fifteen minutes apart and not all that regular and she didn't want me to faint later in the day. So we turned around and went back home to get my two roast beef sandwiches. I found the empty wrappings on the kitchen floor. Our dog Sammler had already made good use of the roast beef. I told Sybil that was okay: at least Sammler wouldn't faint that day.

Back in the car driving to the hospital, we regretted not having a massage vibrator. The Lamaze instructor had said that a battery-operated vibrator would help Sybil relax during labor. I would be able to massage her shoulders and neck and arms while I counted breaths and she focused on mountains and flowing water. In early December, Sybil had driven all over Houston, but the only vibrators she could find were the kind you have to plug in. Finally, someone suggested she inquire at an adult bookstore.

I've always wondered what that fellow in that shop in a sleazy section of Westheimer Street thought when this fully pregnant woman walked in. Pictures of naked women, the kind that help men focus their breathing, covered the walls. Racks of pornographic magazines and videos lined the dimly lit aisles. Instruments of erotica, things you wouldn't know what to do with or where to put, filled the display counters. Into that scene on an ordinary Tuesday afternoon walks a pregnant woman who strides right up to the counter and asks, "Do you sell vibrators?"

"What's that, mam?" The man couldn't focus on the question for puzzling at the questioner. He was used to incongruities, businessmen in eight-hundred-dollar suits asking for the unexpected, but the incongruity between this questioner and her question shocked even his unshakable sense of incongruity.

"Do you sell vibrators?"

"Vibrators?" The poor man was clearly confused. He didn't know whether this woman was an undercover police agent, a new kind of pervert now loosed upon the world, or some sex-crazed maniac the likes of which he had only read about in the magazines he sold. And he thought he had seen everything. "Well . . . yes-um," he finally could reply, "I've got some thangs 'round here that vibrates."

"Thank goodness!" Sybil exclaimed. "You wouldn't believe it: I've been all over Houston looking for a vibrator."

"Well, you come to the right place this time, mam."

"Are they portable?" she asked. "I need a portable vibrator, you know, battery-operated."

"Yes-um, I got some nice-uns that runs on battries."

"Good," she said. "I found plenty that you have to plug in, but this is the first place that has some that are battery-operated."

"Mam," the man reluctantly said, "excuse me for saying so, but you don't exactly look like a candidate for a vibrator. I seen you trying to git outta that car, mam. Mam, you so big you can't hardly walk through the door."

"I know," Sybil laughed. "It's just terrible. My baby's two weeks overdue. That's why I got these slippers on. My feet are too big for all my shoes. I'm just shuffling along. I'm afraid I'm going to get varicose veins. But tell me about your vibrators?"

"Well, whut shape did you have in mind, mam?"

"What do you mean, what shape?"

"You know, mam, we got different sizes and shapes in this store, different colors, too."

"Well, what do you have?"

"Well, mam"—and here the man felt a feeling he sometimes felt but could not name, a feeling of the startling peculiarity of his own situation arising no doubt from the massive gap between what his momma had taught him and what he was doing with his life, standing behind this counter, peddling tawdry sleaze and cheap pleasure for high prices—"well, mam," he continued, "we got three or four kinds."

Sprightly Sybil replied, "Wonderful. I'm going to use one when I have my baby."

The man lost all focus. He could hardly breathe as he whispered, "Whut's that, mam?" The man was concerned about his own mental stability.

Sybil said, "I'm going to use a vibrator when I have my baby. Actually, my husband is going to use it on me."

With his full weight now leaning on the counter, the man replied, "Mam, do I understand curreckly that yor husband is going to use this vibrator on you when you is havin' yor babee?"

"That's right," Sybil said. "Our teacher said it would help me during labor, especially if it goes on too long. And the doctor said it wouldn't hurt. It could last for hours, you know, and it would relax me."

This long-time purveyor of various kinds of materials having to do with relaxing diverse parts of the human anatomy had never encountered such as this.

"Mam," he finally said, "exactly whut kind of teacher wuz that?"

"My Lamaze teacher," Sybil replied. "She said it would help me when I'm in labor to use a vibrator, along with the breathing and the pictures and the music. It'll help my husband, too."

The man had never heard of any brand of "marital aids" called

*Lamaze*. Maybe it was foreign, he thought. In any case, this was one market segment that may be ready for expansion: vibrators for pregnant women. He figured that not even those big shops in New Orleans had thought of that yet. And if the vibrators went over big, maybe they could open up a whole new line of magazines and related devices designed especially for pregnant women, for their husbands, too. He thought that there had to be thousands of babies being born all the time, right in Houston, Texas, and that a lot of pregnant women might be in the market for a good battry-operated vibrator.

"How you spell that name, mam?"

"What name?" Sybil asked.

"You know, the name of your teacher."

"You mean Lamaze?"

"Yes, mam, Lamaze."

"L-a-m-a-z-e."

I never heard exactly how the conversation ended, but Sybil left the store again disappointed: for some reason, she decided that the man's vibrators, even though battery-operated, wouldn't do.

As it turned out, we managed without the roast beef sandwiches and the vibrator, because thirty minutes after getting into the birthing room, Sybil said that she had had enough of nature. She demanded narcotics. The tape and the picture and the breathing didn't do the job. I felt like a failure and knew I must be doing something wrong, but she said she doubted if the vibrator would have done any good either. She told me to tell the nurse to tell the doctor, "Get me something quick."

Standing at the end of the table when Keith Reeves held baby Barrett up for us to see, I forgot all that. All the preparation didn't matter any more. I was aware only of Sybil and of our seeing baby Barrett for the first time.

All fathers say the same thing: there is nothing else like it. To lean over to your wife and say, "Here's our baby." And for her to say, "Yes, that's our baby." There's nothing else like it. There's nothing more one can say. Nothing more one needs to say.

"He's beautiful. And big. He's thirteen pounds, seven ounces." Sybil was in the recovery room talking to her mother on the phone. "Yes. Would you believe it?" she continued. "Thirteen pounds, seven ounces. And thirty-two inches long. I can't believe it."

I hesitantly interrupted to say, "Sybil, I think Barrett is seven pounds, thirteen ounces, not thirteen pounds, seven ounces. And I think the nurse said he is twenty-two inches long, not thirty-two."

"Well, thirteen or thirty-two, it doesn't matter. I can't believe it."

Every parent knows she is right: you can't believe it. It expands your sense of incredulity beyond anything you have known before.

Johann Sebastian Bach wrote thousands of pieces of music and fathered twenty-two children. I've sometimes thought it was all that birth that drove him to write all that music. There's old J. S. Bach, trying with fugues and sonatas and gigues and toccatas and preludes and cantatas and chorales and sarabandes, fanatically writing thousands and thousands of them, seeking all the time to do in music what he could not do in words: give ample voice to his sense of incredulity over each one of those twenty-two babies.

It reminds me of Hannah Arendt. Hannah Arendt was a philosopher, and she argues that natality has precedence over mortality. Birth has precedence over death. It's a shocking claim, really, especially given Arendt's work with Martin Heidegger who talks everywhere about our being-toward-death. That's the situation of human beings for Martin Heidegger: we are being-toward-death, and we had best not forget it, but we invariably do. Arendt learned that from Heidegger, and after she learned it, she spent twenty years thinking about the Holocaust, that wholesale manufacture of death that threatens to blot out any sense of possibility for goodness in life.

But despite all that death and all that thinking about life from the point of death, Arendt seized on natality as fundamental. She said that birth is the great fact. It is the great Yes, the irreducible and inexhaustible Yes by which the No's are to be measured. And when so measured, all the many No's are found unequal to, incommensurate with, the Yes of birth.

On the night of New Year's Day, 1980, on that night I would have had no trouble believing Hannah Arendt. To tell you the truth, it would have taken all the music of Bach and all the elegant arguments of all the Hannah Arendts and I still would not have been able to give ample voice to this fundamental reality: the birth of our baby.

# La Leche

"Hello, Mrs. Estess, I'm calling from the Houston chapter of La Leche League. I understand that you are going to have a baby. Mrs. Estess, that's wonderful, just wonderful. You are going to breastfeed your baby, aren't you?"

Sybil had barely heard of La Leche League, so understandably, the call caught her off guard. She thought it somewhat forward for a perfect stranger to inquire about such a thing, and over the phone, too. Where Sybil grew up, people didn't use the word "breast" in polite conversation. She got it from her mother. One time, when Sybil was nine years old, she asked her mother what the word "pregnant" meant. Her mother said she didn't know. Who knows, maybe she didn't. My mother always said that babies "just came along." Anyway, Sybil was taken aback with the call. "Who are you?" she asked.

"I'm Alma from La Leche League and I'm calling to encourage you to breastfeed. Breastfeeding is nature's way of caring for your baby, you know that, don't you?"

" Well, yes," Sybil said as Alma interrupted.

"I do hope that you will come to our classes. We meet at the First Unitarian Church on Tuesday nights. We want all expectant mothers and fathers to learn about breastfeeding. Can we expect you and your husband on Tuesday night?"

"I don't know if we are free or not," Sybil replied, uncharacteristically adding, "I'll have to check with my husband."

"Listen, Mrs. Estess, I hope you realize how serious this is. You want to be a good mother, don't you?"

"Well, yes," and again Alma interrupted.

"Mrs. Estess, if you don't breastfeed, your baby will not get off to a healthy start. A lot depends on it—his health, intelligence, immune system, digestive system, why, everything depends on it. Studies in France have shown that breastfed babies are 32% more intelligent than formula babies, and they have fewer allergies, too. The mother's milk has the nutrients and everything else that the baby needs to get a good, happy start." With a little giggle, she added, "And you know what, Mrs. Estess, breastfed poop smells better, too. You'll be glad of that when you start changing all those diapers."

Actually, Sybil had thought a great deal about whether she would breastfeed. Like natural childbirth, it was definitely the right thing to do, and she wanted to do the right thing. I myself took some interest in Sybil's breasts during the pregnancy. I told her they seemed to be doing real well and that if an increase in size had anything to do with it, she would do all right with that breastfeeding. That seemed to make her feel better.

One day along about the sixth month of pregnancy, a friend of ours named Candace came to see Sybil and brought her some books, eleven in all, on breastfeeding. Candace said those books had helped her breastfeed her two kids; and since she wasn't going to have any more kids and knew all about breastfeeding anyway, she didn't need the books anymore and wanted Sybil to have them. Candace was not a member of the La Leche League, but I'm sure she could have been if she had wanted to.

I was coming in the front door as Candace was leaving. She asked me to walk with her out to her car. Almost in a whisper, she said, "Ted, I'm concerned about Sybil."

"Why's that, Candace?"

"Ted, I'm not sure she is sold on breastfeeding."

"Well, Candace, I think Sybil wants to breastfeed, you know, if everything goes okay. We've talked about it."

"I know, Ted, but she doesn't seem enthusiastic. You have got to be enthusiastic about breastfeeding if it is really going to be successful, you know that, Ted."

"No, Candace, I don't know too much about breastfeeding—well, I know some, but . . . ." I must admit that I felt uncomfortable standing in front of my house in the broad daylight talking about Sybil's breasts with a woman I barely knew, but Candace was a determined woman.

"Ted, I left Sybil a few books. They will tell her nearly everything she needs to know about breastfeeding. I couldn't have done without them. I want you to read them, too. You can be a big help to Sybil, you know."

"I know, Candace. I'll try."

When I got in the house, Sybil was crying. She said she knew that she wouldn't be able to measure up to Candace's standards for breastfeeding. Sybil showed me all the books that Candace had left. It was a stack over a foot high and included paperbacks and a few hardbacks. I glanced through them and was interested in the pictures of how to hold the baby and position him in relationship to the breast in order to make things easy for the mother and comfortable for the baby and how to maximize the amount of milk that the mother's breasts would produce and the baby would take.

Sybil told me that she didn't think that she would have time to read all those books, but I told her to forget it. I told her that mothers had been breastfeeding their babies for a long time without reading eleven books on the subject and that they seemed to have been doing okay, mothers and babies alike. I told Sybil that I was surprised that Candace didn't leave a book for our baby to read. Still, Sybil was upset, but I assured her that I would help in any way I could.

I did try, especially when we got home from the hospital on Sunday, January 5th. That first week I watched Sybil feed Barrett every chance I got. She would sit down in the rocking chair we had gotten from her mother, the one in which she had rocked Sybil and her sister when they were babies, and I would hand Barrett to Sybil, help her bare her breast, and then I would watch that little fellow suck away, a regular Hoover, he was. I thought Candace would be pleased with me.

After a week with all three of us doing our various parts, Sybil and I took Barrett to the doctor for his first checkup. Our pediatrician had come highly recommended. We had interviewed him before Barrett was born and talked with him about everything we could think of. After the interview, Sybil said she didn't like the gray and white striped railroad engineer's cap that the doctor wore all the time. She said it looked silly. I told her that the engineer's cap went with the electric trains that were winding their way above the nurses' station in the central area off the examining rooms. There must have been two hundred feet of railroad track suspended from the ceiling, and three or four trains going all the time. You could sit in the examining room and watch the trains passing through little villages with all the little houses and stores and churches and stations, and going up and down mountains, through tunnels, and across valleys. Above the chatter of doctors and nurses and parents and the occasional cry of a baby, you could hear the whirl of trains and an occasional toot-toot-toot of a whistle. All that probably helped the babies and pleased the fathers. I know that I liked watching those trains.

"Mmm, let's see how this little fella is doing," Dr. Frank Hill said. His gray and white engineer's cap was pulled down. I had trouble seeing his eyes, but he was determined, no doubt like an engineer trying to get his train across Independence Pass out in Colorado. "Mmm, that's not too good," he said, as if talking to himself. The locomotive went toot-toot-toot as it chugged along outside Dr. Hill's door and entered the tunnel.

"What's that, Dr. Hill?" I asked. Sybil and I were shaky. What could be wrong with our baby? What were we doing wrong?

"He weighs seven-pounds-six-ounces. That's down six ounces from his birth weight. We expect a baby to lose a few ounces, but a week out, this boy should be gaining weight. Is he getting enough to eat?"

"I think so," Sybil said, clearly feeling uneasy.

"Her breasts sure are big enough to be giving enough milk," I added. Sybil's stare at me suggested that perhaps I had said something I ought not to have said.

"Well, you know, Dr. Mr. Estess, breast size doesn't have too much to do with milk production." Out of professional courtesy, I guess, Dr. Hill always called me "Dr. Mr. Estess" and Sybil "Dr. Mrs. Estess." Maybe he thought that would make us feel better about being around a real doctor.

After further consultation, Dr. Hill tilted his engineer's cap back on his head and said, "Here's what I want you to do. I want you to take these scales home, these right here. For the next week or so, I want you to weigh Barrett before you feed him. Weigh him and record the weight. Then feed him. Then weigh him again and record the weight. That way, we'll see exactly how much milk he's getting. I want it to be three or four ounces a feeding in the next week or so."

We walked out the door into a cool January day, Sybil carrying Barrett with his little blue cap and I the shining scales. In the background, we heard the choo-choo train struggling up Independence Pass whistling toot-toot all the way to the top.

That afternoon we started, but right at the outset Sybil and I disagreed on how to proceed. We were, after all, doing something that we had never heard about, much less done before. I told Sybil that it didn't matter what clothes Barrett had on when we fed him just so long as he had the same clothes on when we weighed him after the feeding. She said that with his clothes on we wouldn't know exactly what he weighed. I told her that it didn't matter what he actually weighed. We were interested only in the weight gained with the feeding. She said she would do it my way but felt sure it would be more accurate if we took Barrett's clothes off every time he fed. That way we would know exactly how much he weighed. We agreed to disagree, but I was glad that Sybil acquiesced: I least I wouldn't have to put a naked baby down on those cold, shiny, stainless steel scales.

So there we were, Dr. Mrs. Sybil and Dr. Mr. Ted Estess, two Ph.D.s, following the instructions of Railroad Engineer and Pediatrician Dr. Frank Hill, M.D., weighing the baby, feeding the baby, weighing the baby, every four hours, weighing the baby, feeding the baby, weighing the baby, day and night. Sybil said that it wasn't fair for her both to weigh and feed. If she did the feeding, at least I could get up and do the weighing and keep the records. She said I was better with math than she was anyway.

"Let's see, little fella," I said. "Hold still so I can weigh you." It was 2:45 a.m. that first night of the new regimen. Sybil and I were in Barrett's room, and I was trying to get him weighed. "Let's see, let me get this scale balanced. There, there, Barrett, stop that wriggling. Hold still, now, hold real still for Daddy. Okay, little fella, hold right there, for one second. Let's see, seven pounds, ten-and-a-half ounces. Okay, Sybil," I finally said, "go to it." I handed Barrett over to Sybil and recorded in my notebook, January 12, 1980, 2:45 a.m.: 7 lbs. 10.5 ozs.

Sybil sat in the rocker and hoisted a heavy breast to the puckering mouth of Baby Barrett. He seemed happy and I could understand why. There are some things that need no explanation: you just know them.

I could manage the weighing and the record keeping, but the tough part was figuring out what to do for the twenty minutes or so I had to wait while Barrett was feeding. I wanted to sleep, but I was sure Candace would see that as a sign of insufficient enthusiasm on my part. After all, she had said that the milk production of the mother is adversely affected by an unenthusiastic breastfeeder of a father. But, you know, it's hard to be an enthusiastic breastfeeder at 3 o'clock in the morning.

Sybil and I didn't have energy to talk in the middle of the night, so I usually just sat and watched her and Barrett. To tell the truth, those were good moments—no, better than good, almost sacred—as I sat in silence and watched the good mother give breast to the good baby. For twenty minutes or so in the deep quiet of the night, everything, I mean everything, seemed okay as those two did what they seemed fully to have come into the world to do. Had I thought about it, I would have been sure that the philosopher Hannah Arendt was right: natality takes precedence over mortality.

"All rightee," I said, taking Barrett from Sybil. "Let's see how much this little fella weighs after getting all that good milk." We hovered over the scales like archaic people fanning the embers of a new fire, squinting to see how he and Sybil's breasts had done. "Okay, Barrett, hold still while Daddy reads these scales. Let's see. Just a second. Okay. There. Seven pounds, twelve-and-three-quarters." Handing Barrett back to Sybil, I said, "What's the gain? Seven pounds, ten-and-one-half from seven pounds, twelve-and-three-quarters. He got two-and-a-quarter ounces. Sybil. He got two-and-a-quarter ounces." I recorded the time, pre-feeding weight, post-feeding weight, and the difference in my log.

One problem we had was deciding whether to weigh Barrett before we burped him or after. We figured the burp must weigh something and ought to be taken into account. We thought about weighing him before and after a burp to determine just how much a burp weighs, but I told Sybil that burps probably differ in weight and the scales may not be that sensitive anyway. After all, how much can a burp weigh? We never considered the problem of a fart, but *mutatis mutandis*, I figured the same would apply to any gaseous emission, whether fart or burp or any other.

This reminds me of an evening a couple of years later when I was bathing young Barrett and he happened to break wind in the bath water, sending airy bubbles dancing happily to the surface. Working already to insure that my clearly precocious child would develop a good vocabulary, I asked, "Are you flatulent?" "No," he replied, "I am Barrett." It occurs to me now that if I had some device to measure the displacement of water, I might have been able to determine how much a fart or a burp weighed, but then, I probably would have had to hold Baby Barrett under water to make the measurement, which would have bothered Sybil.

Sybil and I went on like that for a week. After conferring by phone with Dr. Hill, we continued for a second week, every four hours, weighing and feeding and weighing. After the second week, we returned to the pediatrician's office à la railroad station. First off, Dr. Hill inspected my records. "Dr. Mr. Estess," he said, "you've done a good job keeping these records, a real good job. Some of the best I've ever seen, Dr. Mr. Estess." I felt proud and knew that Candace and Alma from La Leche would be pleased with me.

Looking over my tallies, Dr. Hill continues, "Let's see here, how much milk is this boy getting from Dr. Mrs. Estess? Let's see. He's getting two, sometimes three ounces every feeding. That won't do, that just won't do."

"But, Dr. Hill," Sybil lamented, "that's all I can give. What am I doing wrong?"

"Nothing," the doctor-railroad engineer said, "so forget it. Put him on formula."

"Dr. Hill," I said, "what about his immunities? And his mental development? And won't his poop smell worse? I don't know if I can stand it if it smells any worse than it does now, Dr. Hill."

"Dr. Mr. Estess," he said, "it won't matter a bit whether this baby is on the breast or on the bottle. He'll do fine either way."

"But Dr. Hill," I protested as he interrupted me.

"Listen—you too Dr. Mrs. Estess—I've got nine children of my own and I know something about these things. Some of my children were breast-babies, some were bottle-babies. I can't remember which was which. It doesn't matter. Forget breastfeeding and buy some bottles. Use those plastics ones they've got now. You don't have to do all that washing."

Sybil and I left Dr. Frank Hill's office that day with slumped shoulders. We had failed. La Leche League and Candace would be disappointed in us. We thought that if Dr. Hill was right and it didn't matter, what the hell had we been doing getting up at all hours of the night weighing that baby, anyway. As it turned out, he was right about everything but the poop: it did smell worse.

# Fishing Spirit Lake

"Dad," Barrett said, "let's hike up to one of the high mountain lakes. They say the fishing is really good up there."

Barrett's suggestion surprised me. Usually my thirteen-year old son says he hates walking. I was pleased but also concerned. A hike to the high lakes is strenuous and you need to be in shape. I am not in shape.

"That would be great, Barrett," I said. "The closest I know is Lone Pine Lake."

"Is the fishing good?" he asked.

"I would think so. It's about six miles up the East Inlet Trail. I doubt many people get up that far to fish."

"Are you sure? I want to catch fish. Are there any lakes higher up?"

"Well, we could go a couple of miles further to Lake Verna and Spirit Lake."

"We'll go to Spirit Lake," he announced.

It was settled, just like that. Both of us would get what we wanted. I would get a hike with my son and he would get fish. A fifteen, almost sixteen, mile round-trip might be a bit long, but I wasn't about to say a discouraging word.

So on Sunday morning Sybil dropped us at East Inlet Trailhead at the end of Grand Lake. Barrett complained we were getting a late start. It was 6:15.

From the outset I recalled making the same hike two years ago to Lone Pine, which is one of four glacier lakes that sit in the lap of Mount Baldy. I went alone then and spent a good deal of the day thinking about a college friend named Harrison Kohler and how he almost got himself killed in Vietnam but got back. I had my guidebook to Western wildflowers along then and stopped to identify some along the trail. I especially liked the lupines. They reminded me of bluebonnets in Texas.

"Come on, Dad. Pick up the pace. We'll never get there at this rate." For the first of about a hundred times, Barrett used the words "pick up the pace." He seemed to derive from them the same kind of sadistic pleasure that drill instructors have in barking orders to recruits at Marine boot camp.

"Pick up the pace, Dad."

"We're going fast enough, Barrett."

"No, we're not. I don't want to fish Lone Pine. I want to fish Verna and then Spirit Lake. It's seven miles to Verna, almost eight to Spirit. We can make it to Verna in two-and-a-half hours."

"Barrett," I said, "there's a 1900-foot elevation rise on this trail."

"So?"

"So we're going up."

"So we're going up," he repeated. "What's the big deal?"

"The big deal is that this is hard work."

"Dad, I want to be fishing at 10 o'clock. Pick up the pace."

That's pretty much the way it went. Barrett kept insisting we speed up. I kept insisting we were going fast enough. I couldn't go any faster.

Barrett had no trouble walking and talking at the same time. He ranged across movies, music, friends, school, and sports, endlessly he talked.

A son can never appreciate the pleasure a father receives from hearing his son's voice. My taking pleasure in Barrett's voice had to be enough, because I couldn't keep up my end of the conversation except for an occasional grunt or brief question. You have to be able to control your breathing to talk, and I started panting about a half-mile up the trail, just above Adams Falls.

"I've been waiting for ten minutes," Barrett said, as I flopped down on the rock beside him.

"Thanks for waiting," I wheezed. My chest heaved. My legs ached.

"We'll never make it like this, Dad," he said. "It's nearly 8 o'clock and we haven't gone three miles, have we?"

"Three miles in less than two hours up a trail like this is pretty good, son."

"Dad, we won't have but a few hours to fish. You'll want to head back by 3 o'clock."

"Listen, son," I said, "people my age die doing things like this. I don't care how much time we have to fish. I just want to make it to Lone Pine Lake."

"Dad, I told you I want to go to Spirit Lake. It's only two miles beyond Lone Pine."

"We can talk about that later. First, we've got to get to Lone Pine. That's another three miles from here." I trudged past him. Over my shoulder I asked, "Say, Barrett, do you know CPR?"

"What's CPR?" he asked.

By now we were moving beyond the Lodge Pole pines and into Engelman spruce and Douglas firs. The spruce glimmered in the broken light of a partially cloudy day. Most of them were small, not over ten and fifteen feet. The firs were grand, especially along the streams that regularly crossed the trail. Here and there we moved through a grove of aspen. "What's that smell?" Barrett asked. "It's terrible." He had waited for me again, and I was glad to catch up.

"That's smoke," I said. "Haven't you noticed the fire damage? We've been in it for three hundred yards." I pointed above the trail to the burned over region. A band of aspen was charred and still reeking with the stench of smoke. "It looks like the trail helped the firefighters contain the fire," I said. "See, the fire jumped the trail only in one place, right back there."

"I didn't see that," Barrett replied. "I just knew that something around here stinks."

The difference between us was clear: he wanted to catch fish; I wanted to take a walk with him.

Maybe that's the way it has to be with parents and kids: parents are ancillary to what kids have in mind. We resist and complain and ask them to consider others, especially us. But we lose out and end up serving whatever projects the kids devise. We thus are disposable, to be used for a while, and then to be left behind as surely as Barrett left me yesterday morning on the side of Mount Baldy.

Kids don't serve any purpose for parents other than to be kids. I huff about expecting this or that from Barrett, but it's a show: he's enough in himself, at least for me, and he knows it. He doesn't have to do much of anything. I'll be satisfied. He can disappoint me, but my regard for him will not change. It is unconditional. Well, almost.

"Dad," Barrett said as we moved across one of the steepest parts of the trail. It was already 8:45. We were still a ways from Lone Pine Lake, but had made five miles in two-and-a-half hours. Not bad on a steep trail. "Dad, it just occurred to me: I might not catch any fish today."

"That's right," I huffed. "You might not."

"I tell you what, Dad. I'm going to be really pissed off if I don't catch any fish."

I'm uncomfortable with my son using such an inelegant expression, but I didn't correct him. Let him use words proper to the occasion, I thought. He was right: he is always pissed off if he doesn't catch any fish.

"Will you?" I replied.

"You're damn right, Dad. I'll be pissed off. This will be an incredible waste of a day if I don't catch any fish, I mean, a hell of a lot of fish."

Again ignoring the infelicity of speech, I gasped, "We'll see."

Another few turns on the switchback and I had to stop again. Even Barrett seemed content to stop for a drink of water. "Barrett," I said, "I've been thinking of something that Saint Teresa said."

"Who's that?"

"Saint Teresa of Avila. She was a mystic, a holy woman in Spain six or seven hundred years ago. She had visions and the Pope made her a saint."

"Well, what did she say?"

She said, "It's heaven all the way to heaven, and it's hell all the way to hell."

"Say that again."

"It's heaven all the way to heaven, and it's hell all the way to hell."

"I don't understand," he said.

"I can't explain it."

"Why not?" he asked.

"It's one of those things that—"and he interrupted me to take over the sentence.

"I know," he said. In a tone mocking me, he added, "'It's one of those things that you to have to know before someone can explain it.' Dad, why do you always say that?"

"I don't always say that. I say it only when it fits. There are just some things you somehow have to know before somebody else can explain them."

"Dad, that's doesn't make any sense."

"I think it does."

"But if that's true," Barrett said, "how will I ever know what Saint-whoever-she-was meant."

"When you need to," I answered.

"What do you mean?"

"I mean you will know what it means when you need to know it."

"That doesn't make any sense either. But tell me, Dad. If it's heaven all the way to heaven, and it's hell all the way to hell, what is it right now, right now on this hike? You tell me: is this heaven or hell?"

"I'm not sure," I panted.

"OOOO-KKKK," Barrett said, standing up. "Enough of that stuff, let's go." He backed down below me on the trail and said, "Here, Dad, let me give you a push." He placed both his hands on my butt and started pushing me up the mountain.

"Barrett, that's great," I said. "Amazing," I shouted, as my breath returned. I was a blocking dummy in football practice: he was shoving me along. I felt fifty pounds lighter.

"That's enough, man," he said, after a hundred yards or so. This summer Barrett has taken to calling me man. "Okay, man," he will say. I don't know what this change means, but man is not the same as Dad. "You go ahead, man," he continued. "Go way on up. I want you to see me run up the hill. Here, man, take my backpack."

"No way, man," I said. "I'm lucky to carry my own backpack."

I moved up the mountain without benefit of Barrett's posterior propulsion. I still felt lighter from the push. I hiked a hundred yards or so, well into the rock field, and remembered those grayish granite rocks from two years ago. I wrote to my friend Harrison and told him they reminded me of a bombed out region, something like he must have seen in Vietnam. It's moon-like, eerie and intimidating, all that geologic debris pulled haphazardly by an avalanche down the craggy face of the mountain.

I turned down the trail to see Barrett racing up across the rock field. His red backpack bounced above his shoulders. His stride looked two yards long as he bore toward me. It was as amazing as anything I saw all day, my son striding up that trail like an antelope. I was frightened, thinking his heart might burst with the strain. I read in the paper just last week about a well-conditioned basketball player falling over dead after a pickup game in Salt Lake City. I wanted to tell Barrett to slow down, don't over do it, but I was struck dumb by the sight of this lanky youngster leaping grayish rocks, bounding toward me.

"How's that, man?" he asked, as he bent over to breathe.

"That's great," I said. "I don't know how you did it."

"You didn't think I could run that far, did you? I could have gone further."

Barrett stood for a minute, and I found myself doing what the old are bound to do: I resented his youth and energy, his victory over the mountain. My resentment turned to thought: *He is no happier, no more accomplished*, I thought, *in his youth than I was in mine, and maybe less. Compared to me at his age, he has traveled more and read more books, seen more baseball games, and caught more fish. But I was more self-sufficient and less dependent on being entertained. I could bear silence and didn't mind being alone. I could milk a cow and play the piano and hammer a nail and paint a house and stand up and give a talk. I knew how to pray and didn't sass my mother. I could work all day and do things I didn't want to do just because I had to do them. I loved Chopin. I don't remember whining, and I didn't know what the word bored meant. When I was thirteen and saw these same mountains for the first time, I stood and gawked until my eyes hurt. Why*, I thought, *doesn't he?*

"Come on, man," Barrett said. "Pick up the pace. We gotta make it to Lone Pine by 9:30." We picked our way through the rocks, those grayish-whitish-deadish-moonscape rocks.

I thought it would be good to rest under the huge firs at Lone Pine Lake as I did two years ago and eat an apple. I could use my favorite knife, the one I've had for twenty years to carve the apple and clean a few fish if we caught some keepers. Two years ago Lone Pine jumped with fish.

But Barrett insisted we keep moving, so we turned up the trail, on toward Spirit Lake, another two miles and another hour up. He left me about the time the trail ran into the mountain. "Unimproved Trail" the map said for that stretch of the way, and it was. I lost sight of him among the trees and through the boulders.

I didn't mind: I knew the justification for his day lay ahead. It was all out ahead of him, the very reason for his coming to the mountain was yet to be. It was almost 11 o'clock and we had walked eight miles and his day had not begun to happen. Everything that preceded his arrival at Spirit Lake was to be gotten rid of as fast as possible. It was like his life: it wasn't happening yet. It had not begun, not his life, not his day.

My day was already sufficient. I didn't need anything more. I would push on to Spirit Lake, but I was pleased to have made it again to Lone Pine and with my son to boot. I didn't need a fish.

By mid-afternoon, Barrett had no reason to be pissed off. Thirty-nine Brook trout, that's what we caught. We released them all. Barrett had a yen to stay at Spirit Lake until we had landed forty-two. That way he could break the record of forty-one he set a few years ago with his grandfather "Racehorse" Cochran. I told him that thirty-nine should stand as his personal record because that other time Racehorse caught most of the Blue-gills. This time Barrett did most of the catching.

Time and rain ran us off Spirit Lake. With a light rain falling, we packed it in at around 5:30. I wanted to be off the trail before complete darkness fell and we got too wet. Even with my orange poncho on, I could feel the dampness getting through.

Barrett caught a lot more fish than I because he spent more time at it and because he is a better fisherman. He takes risks. I don't. I throw my fly to the open water where there is little chance of getting hung up. Barrett likes the edges, under the rocks or alongside the willows and submerged logs. Sometimes he misses and gets snared on a log or a branch. Several times I watched him scrambling around a stretch of water, balancing on rocks and logs, moving through the river willows, trying to get to a point from which he could free his fly without breaking the line. I told him his mother would be mad if he got his feet wet, but he kept on going. Fifteen minutes before we quit, he stepped into a marsh and got mud and water over the top of his boots. Both feet were soaked, but he said it didn't bother him.

"Coming down is much worse than going up, Dad, much worse."

"Not for me," I answered.

"Yes, it is, Dad. Coming down, you don't have anything to look forward to." We had passed Lone Pine Lake and the rock field and

Slippery Rock camping area. But another five miles lay ahead of us, and it was already 6:30.

"Going up," Barrett said, "I thought about catching fish. That took my mind off walking. Going down, all you got to look forward to is getting back home. There's nothing to do at home."

"I feel great coming down," I said. "I feel great because we made it all the way to Spirit Lake. I wasn't sure I could make it eight miles up this mountain."

"Oh, man, you knew you could make it."

"No, I didn't."

"I don't know what's the big deal about walking eight miles," he said.

"And going down is good," I said, "because I can think about watching you catch all those fish. I like to watch you catch fish."

"That's good," he agreed, "yeah, that's good. It was the best fishing I ever had."

"Better than Magnolia Lake with Papaw?" I asked.

"Yeah, better than that. I was fishing with worms then. Papaw used a fly. Today I used a fly and that's more fun. And trout are more fun to catch than bream, they just are."

We dropped into a stretch of silence as you always do on a long hike. The light rain continued and I liked its tingle on my face. I thought of John Updike and how many of his characters take pleasure in rain. They drive through it, and get out and walk around in it. They turn their faces up to it. One says, "We do love being touched from above—by rain, by snow."

"You go ahead, Dad, and pick up the pace." I don't know where the energy came from, but I found myself half-jogging down the trail. I found it easier letting go into gravity's force and allowing my own corpulence to carry me downhill. For a good mile, I skipped ahead, deftly (for me) moving my feet among the rocks. The switchbacks were fun going down. A couple of times Barrett stumbled and had trouble keeping up.

By 7:15 the rain stopped and we came to the towering rock ledge that presides over the meadow. I recalculated our ETA and told Barrett we would reach the trailhead by 8:30, maybe 8:45. We had less than three miles to go, but I didn't want to hurry now. The mountain and valley and everything in it had been refreshed by rain.

I told Barrett to stop for a preview of what was ahead. We walked over to the ledge and looked down on the lush meadow stretching two miles westward to Grand Lake. Looking across the meadow, Barrett and I saw Grand Lake and the sun dropping behind the hills. For the rest of the day we would be walking in the afterlife of sunset.

"Dad," Barrett said after another thirty minutes of silence, "the worst thing about coming down is thinking you are almost there when you're not."

"I know what you mean," I said. By now we had settled into a steady pace and the trail was wide enough to accommodate the two of us side by side. At one point, Barrett broke off and walked over to get a good look at East Inlet Creek where it broadens and slows down in the flatness of the meadow. I was afraid he might want to start fishing again, but he only said he wanted to come back there and try his luck another day.

"I would like to have another long hike before we leave Colorado," I said, "another one like this."

"I don't know about that, man," he said. "I don't know if I want to do this again or not."

"We'll see," I said. "Say, what time did we tell Mother we would be back?"

"You said around 8. But how will she know when we get there?"

"I told her we would walk into town and call."

"Dad," Barrett exclaimed. "That's another mile at least. You mean we have to walk another mile into town?"

"Maybe Mother will come to meet us," I said. "Let's hope she's at the trailhead waiting for us."

"Man, I hope so."

Passing through the long stretch of meadow, Barrett took hold of my elbow and held lightly to my sleeve. I wasn't sure whether he was letting me escort him down the trail or whether he wanted, so late in the day, to protect his old man against a fall. Maybe he wanted to walk by my side, the two of us together.

"Dad, look at that."

"Incredible," I said.

"That's beautiful, man." We stood quiet for a minute or two. "Mom would love that, wouldn't she, Dad?"

"She really would," I said.

"Dad, look. There are two."

A full double rainbow stretched the length of the meadow. I usually live in the Lone Star State, but I don't know what they call this one. Maybe they call it the Rainbow State. In three weeks we've seen five or six stunning ones. Last Sunday we saw a double over Shadow Mountain Lake. With so many, you would think they would become commonplace.

But rainbows never become commonplace, not double ones, anyway.

"Tell me when we get close to the end, man. I want to run the last half-mile."

"Then, man," I said, "you had better start running right now."

He let go of my arm and took off down the trail, oblivious to the fifteen miles he had already covered and forgetful of fish, fatigue, and his father. The last thing I saw through the trees was a red backpack and a shock of blond hair catching the fading rays of reflected light. Earlier I had wondered whether he had blisters from walking in wet shoes. Now he was running away from me. I thought I might catch a glimpse of him from the next rise in the trail.

I stopped and turned for a last look across the meadow at Mount Baldy. It's notorious in these parts at sunset. Baldy is rightly named. It is a massive, bare rock mountain, stark and grand in its austerity. It scowls. But yesterday, Baldy glowed deeply iridescent, beyond red, nearly crimson. It seemed that the source of the glow was not reflected sunlight off the clouds but light internal to the mountain itself, so radiantly it shone.

I walked in alone thinking about getting back to the cabin. I didn't want to walk another mile to a telephone in town. I hoped Sybil would come on to meet us, and figured she might. She would be anxious to see us and to hear how it all went, whether Barrett caught fish and whether I made the hike okay. I didn't want to tell her that I had let Barrett get his feet wet and maybe blistered.

As the trail dropped below Adams Falls, I heard her voice through the dark. She was there, waiting for us.

# Losing What You Love and Getting It Back Again

## I

Yesterday afternoon I hiked to Lone Pine Lake and spent a good deal of the time thinking about my friend Harrison Kohler.

Beginning at the end of Grand Lake, which is the largest natural lake in Colorado, the trail moves generally eastward, first by Adams Falls, then through East Meadow, on up toward Lone Pine, which sits at about 11,000 feet beneath Mount Baldy.

For much of the way, the trail borders East Inlet Creek. When it does break off, you move into the trees, first Aspen and Lodge Pole pine, but further on, Blue and Englemann spruce, and Balsam fir. The loggers call Balsam fir *piss fir*. They say it smells like piss when you cut it. Leaving the creek, you climb the mountain on the south side of the valley, along a narrow trail.

I hurried going in. Lone Pine Lake is almost six miles from the trailhead and I had a late start. Perhaps I could make the lake in three hours. I stopped once for water and a pack of crackers, and pushed on. At one point the trail moves against a wall of rock and presses the hiker hard against the edge of the cliff.

Passing through dense forest at about 10,000 feet, the trail broke into a huge bowl on the side of the mountain. That's when Harrison Kohler came to mind, why, I'm not sure, but he was with me for the rest of the day. Memory works that way: it gives what it will, when it will. It's a way of getting back something we lost.

Harry, I thought, must have seen something like this in Vietnam, where bombs took away sides of mountains. Over hundreds of acres, thousands of huge trees were snapped off, uprooted and strewn around.

It looked like somebody big had been playing pick-up-sticks.

Coming out of the bowl, the trail leveled off into dense timber again. And there at the base of Mount Baldy was Lone Pine Lake, no more than a hundred acres of green, brilliantly colored by minerals that were churned up by the glacier a million years ago, but muted under the cloudy skies of this late afternoon.

It brought to mind something my father said the first time our family saw the Rockies. On the Fourth of July in 1955 my family drove from Fort Collins, Colorado, up Big Thompson Canyon and into Rocky Mountain National Park. We stopped at Forest Canyon Overlook on Trail Ridge Road, four lowlanders with Mississippi mud between our toes; and we gawked out at Mount Ida and Mount Julian at almost 13,000 feet, with Arrowhead and Inkwell lakes, glistening emerald below. As we stood there, slack-jawed and mute, Ansel Estess, in his soft, melodious, southern tones, said, "Yep, these mountains will be here a long time after I'm gone."

The Estess family had driven fifteen hundred miles under azure skies, and finally we were standing all together to gaze at purple mountains majesty on the Fourth of July, and that was all Ansel Estess could say? "Yep, these mountains will be here a long time after I'm gone."

Yesterday, sitting there beside Lone Pine Lake at the base of Mount Baldy, I finally understood what the man was talking about. It only took me forty years.

Going down was more treacherous. Several times I slipped on wet rocks; but headed home, I saw a good deal more. The lichen differentiated on the rocks: it's not all the same, if you stop to look. The wildflowers were abundant, blue columbine, white clover, aspen daisy, larkspur, and more. I don't know where they were earlier in the day.

About an hour down from the top, I reached to check if my knife was in my pocket. This knife—I call it "Old Crafty"—and my boots have been with me since 1975. In the Bitterroot Mountains and Glacier Park in Montana, alongside Coulter Bay in the Tetons, up Wolf Creek in Yosemite, up Black Mountain at the side of Lake George and across many other Adirondack trails, these boots and this knife have traveled with me. They are old friends, dependable, there when you need them, even if once a year. But the boots could use new soles, and I fear losing Old Crafty. During a hike, I obsessively check to see that it is there.

## Fishing Spirit Lake

In one of his letters from Vietnam, Harrison Kohler told me how the men in Charlie Company had to be careful with all the stuff they hated to carry, and how every day a soldier had to keep the same routine and guard against the unexpected. Harry was the company medic and said that he was outraged when men came to him seeking help for trouble that was of their own making. "Doc, can't you help me out?" one soldier asked. "You idiot," Harry said, "if you hadn't been so goddamn careless, you wouldn't have crotch rot."

Old Crafty was not in my pockets or in the pack. Perhaps it fell out, or perhaps I left it by the lake when I carved an apple. Should I go back to look? It was growing late and the weather could turn worse, and I probably wouldn't find it anyway.

Walking on down, I couldn't think of anything but Old Crafty. I could hear Harry Kohler saying, "Estess, you idiot, can't you keep up with your gear?" With gentler words, I harangue my son Barrett about this kind of carelessness. I told myself that there are other knives in the stores, but a new one would not be the same. Someday, Barrett would have had this knife.

Further down the mountain, I sat down on a rock and Old Crafty poked me in the butt. I never put my knife in my back pocket, but I did yesterday.

Everything came back with the knife. The water descending out of Lone Pine Lake rumbled deep from the mountains, a *basso profoundo* two miles to the east. The meadow with its meandering creek spread splendidly out below. And from the west, the higher pitched sounds of Adams Fall, tremulant in the evening air, drifted up the valley.

During the hike in, everything held together and comprised one grand vista, the mountains, the creek, the meadow, and the lake. But now, the parts of the scene stuck out from the whole. Everywhere, fragments of wood, shards of rock, and debris of various kinds lay tossed together, interspersed. The landscape seemed all in pieces, each thing discrete, even special, asking for my attention.

At one point in the meadow, the trail turned away from the creek and edged up to the base of the mountain. Up ahead a doe and her fawn crossed, going toward the meadow to graze for the night. A stretch of wetland lay alongside the trail, cut off from the meadow beyond. Back home, folks might call this stretch a swamp, but here it is a slough, like John Bunyan's "slough of despond." Moose like this place.

Rejoining the creek, I passed Adams Falls again, barely able to hear the voices of the few souls who had come at late evening to see the cascade. My car was a welcomed sight at the edge of Grand Lake.

In the village, I stopped for a paper. I was ready for some news and wanted to check the baseball scores. Some young people crossed in front of me and went into Old Grumpy's, a lively bar on main street. One young woman had on a Notre Dame sweatshirt and tight white shorts hiked high on the thigh.

It would be nice to stop in and have a beer or two. I could ask her how the Irish were going to do this year. But I knew it would be no good: I was feeling grumpy and old myself.

So I headed home to our rented cabin on Sun Valley Lake. I was glad to see Sybil and Barrett. They seemed glad to see me, too.

## II

The hike the other day put in mind the experience of losing things and getting them back. Maybe it was the knife. Or maybe, at the end of the day, I got Sybil and Barrett back, and they me. They've been lost to me for a stretch, but walking in the door, we were here again, together. That's one reason to get away: it helps you get your home back.

Now and again, the experience of getting someone back is so strong it is as if you are seeing her for the first time. It is like coming back from the dead. You wipe the dust of the grave from your eyes, look around, and say, "You really are beautiful, you know?"

And it is like that trip to Colorado my family made in 1955. Getting back to Mississippi in early August, and finally crossing the Walthall County line, my taciturn father broke his silence to announce, "Well, boys, we went four thousand miles, but we didn't see anything as pretty as Walthall County, Mississippi."

For several weeks, folks would stop my father on Beulah Avenue—that's main street in Tylertown, Mississippi, my hometown—and ask him about our trip. My father did not mention the wheat fields of Kansas or the mountains of Colorado or the Garden of the Gods or Bear Lake. With

## Fishing Spirit Lake

everybody, he got right to the point: "I tell you what, my friend, we went four thousand miles but we didn't see anything as pretty as Walthall County, Mississippi."

By whatever measure, any one of a hundred streams here in Colorado is more beautiful than Magee's Creek alongside which Tylertown sits. Magee's Creek is renowned only for muscadine vines and water moccasins; and whatever its charms, Walthall County would not strike an impartial observer as Beulah Land, even if folks there refer to it as the "Cream Pitcher of Mississippi." Why then does my father make audacious claims for his little postage stamp of earth? Do others feel the same way about their home place, wherever it happens to be?

Millions do. Why?

This feeling arises, I think, from losing something and getting it back. My father has lived in Walthall County long enough to have lost it and gotten it back hundreds of times. On occasion when he gets it back, it is like having it for the first time. It is all the more dear. Maybe none of us really prize anything until we lose it and get it back again.

Some years ago, I lost everything, or thought I had. Harrison Kohler happened to be in Houston attending a course where prosecutors study better ways to send crooks to jail. It was June, and I was despondent and scared. Other than that, I was in great shape. But I had forgotten it for a while.

I've had four such bouts with deep-down *melancholia* now, and don't want to have another if I can help it. They mess up my day and bother Sybil.

The first was a real embarrassment for me and a source of some discomfort for Sybil. We were going to be married in August of 1966, about the time Harry Kohler was taking off for Vietnam. Harry told me he was not as scared going to Vietnam as I was getting married. But then he said he was only going to war: I was taking a wife.

That summer before Sybil and I married, I caught a terror. Understandably, Sybil thought my terror had something to do with her. After several decades of marriage, she knows better. Now if I catch a terror, she lets me be terrorized on my own time. Don't bother her: she has problems enough of her own. But back then she was young and inexperienced in matrimonial matters. If I happened to catch a sour stomach, she thought she had done something wrong or that there was a problem with our "rela-shun-ship." Maybe we should see a marriage counselor. Now she goes her merry way and I take Alka-Seltzer.

But in July of 1966, a month before the wedding, I was anxious, depressed, and generally not feeling well. Perhaps I didn't love her. Perhaps I was certifiably crazy. Looking back, I would put some credence in the second of these hypotheses, but not the first. I was crazy, but I loved her quite a bit, certainly as best I could at the time, which caused me to be serious about that wedding.

I can't pretend, even now, to understand much about what was going on inside me, but I had lost Sybil for a while. I had lost myself as well. Maybe it was a good sign. A young man who gets married without being scared doesn't understand much.

But Sybil was understandably concerned; so she called in the marriage counselors; and, of course, they were as mystified as she. Various experts pronounced various and conflicting opinions about the young groom to be. "Well, I tell you, young lady," one said to Sybil—I was sitting in the room, too, listening to him—"he's a bad risk. Chuck him while you can." Another avowed that it was probably okay for Sybil and me to go ahead. "He's a serious young man," he said, "but he'll get over it."

I did get over it. About the time I said "I do," I was as happy as a new dollar bill. I had gotten her back again, as had she me. Sybil was the most beautiful bride, and I was a tolerable groom, even if my tux pants were two inches too short. The first time Barrett saw our wedding pictures, he said, "Mom, I didn't know you were a princess." He said that I looked like a clown. After some punch with globs of lime sherbet floating around in it and a piece of wedding cake, we left the Baptist Church in Poplarville, Mississippi, and drove thirty-two miles north for the first night of an elegant honeymoon at the Holiday Inn on Highway 49 in Hattiesburg and started finding ourselves together—making ourselves, too. We haven't stopped yet.

But that June when Harry Kohler came to Houston, he found me in the dumps again. One evening he was with Sybil and me in our dining room when I started to cry. It did not make for an graceful dinner. The broccoli got cold, and I served up despondency. I was up to my elbows in the slough of despond.

# Fishing Spirit Lake

I feel like a clown now when I contemplate my distress. It shows again that what's happening outside you often has little connection with what's happening inside. Outside, things were fine, but inside I was like that bowl of rocks and debris I passed through on the way up to Mount Baldy. I was all parts. My stomach was in Havana, my head in Oshkosh, and my liver in Poughkeepsie. I didn't know where I was. Nowhere, I guess.

That evening in our dining room, against all reason and all objective calculation, I felt as though I had lost everything. Harry gave me a big bear hug, right there before God and everybody, and said, "I'm sorry, Ted. I wish you didn't feel so bad." He allowed how he expected things eventually to turn out all right, which they did. It took a few months, but I got everything back again, except the time I had spent thinking I had lost everything.

Some days now I sit at the piano in our living room and look across and on through the hallway and dining room to the window at the west side of the house. The afternoon light comes softly through the trees into that window and illumines everything. Every single thing stands out, the table and the chairs, the rug, each book in the case. The cracks above the doors don't bother me, and I don't mind the scars on the floor. It all seems good, as though made for me. I feel like Adam felt when he saw things for the first time: "Hey, look at that," he said one morning. "That's a tiger. And that. That's a three-toed East African pilianthropod."

I am talking about Adam after the Fall, after he got the knowledge of good and evil. That's when he wised up and thought he had lost everything. That must be how Adam and Eve felt after they ate that apple, or whatever it was, and got kicked out of the Garden, knowing for the first time they were going to die. They must have felt at least as bad as I felt when I fell into the slough of despond in Houston, Texas.

But once outside the Garden, Adam got some things back, not everything, but some things. Having lost so much, he wanted to see every single thing. Eve, too.

The desire to see every single thing arises, in part, from thinking that you have lost, or will lose, everything. That's what bouts with melancholia have done to me. Of course, I have never actually lost everything, but I have had the actual feeling of having done so. When you are off the trail and in a slough, this is a distinction without a difference.

It's like something that happened during my first year in college, during something they called Religious Emphasis Week. It now seems strange that the good folks at Baylor University would set aside a whole week to emphasize religion, since that was one of the few things my friends and I paid any attention to anyway.

I could have used a Religious De-emphasis Week, and so could have my friends Harry Kohler and Hardy Jones and Houston Craighead. The last time I saw Hardy Jones was in Fort Worth on New Year's Day of 1976. He told me that one night Craighead came up to his room on the fifth floor of Brooks Hall. Harry Kohler was there, too. Craighead was by then a senior philosophy major, intent on practicing language analysis on unsuspecting ministerial students, which meant that Craighead subjected all propositions to that criterion of validity set forth by A. J. Ayers in his book *Language, Truth and Logic,* namely, that only those propositions are valid that are either empirically verifiable or analytically the case. A claim is analytically the case if it is true by definition, for example, 2+2=4.

As applied by Houston Craighead this criterion of validity pretty well wiped out about 98% of all the things a young Baptist preacher boy like Hardy Jones wanted to say. Craighead took after Jones, interrogating his beliefs and carving them to pieces. When Craighead finished, Jones' and his beliefs were a pile of disconnected skin and bones. Finally, Jones, at least what was left of him, cowered in the closet to escape the bitter attack. Without a touch of irony, Craighead shouted his final indictment through the closet door: "I'll tell you what's wrong with you, Jones, I'll tell you what's wrong with you. Jones, you haven't worked out your . . . your Christology."

So during Religious Emphasis Week in February of 1961, I went blithely over to chapel on a Wednesday morning and sat down in my assigned seat, ready with twelve hundred other Baylor freshmen to hear someone else emphasize religion. To that point in my confused life, a considerable part of religion was what many Baptists had told me it was, namely, preparation for life in another world. The question was, Is there life after death and, if so, how to be sure that one would get in on it. But that very February day 1961, my eyes were opened to see that the question is not whether there is life after death. The question is whether there is life after birth.

The religious emphasizer that day was a crazy man named Joseph Schichler, or something like that. Schichler had come down from Chicago to form an existentialist religious community in the hills outside of Austin. For a while, Schichler tried to give despair a good name, which is hard to do in Texas.

There I was, half asleep, preoccupied with the pleats in the skirt of the coed sitting next to me. I was orbiting through the deep space of my own interior galaxies, when Schichler starting shouting something about Lazarus in the tomb. At the top of his voice, right there in Waco Hall, he screamed, "Come out of there, Lazarus. Come on out of there." I couldn't figure it out, but somehow he seemed to be talking to me. Then Schichler fell down, flat out on the floor. I raised up from my seat to see what the crazy man was going to do next. He had made so much racket, and now everything was so quiet, I thought he might have died right there. Lifting his head just off the stage floor, Schichler screamed even louder, "Come out of there, Lazarus. Come on out of there."

Picture it, young man Lazarus, freshly dead and thinking he is through with his busy-body sisters and his disappointed wife. Finally getting some rest, he hears a crazy man shouting through the door, "Come out of there, Lazarus. Come on out of there." So he gets up, comes to the door, wipes his eyes, and looks around. "My, my," he says, "I haven't seen that before." Even his disappointed wife didn't seem disappointing that night.

# III

Yesterday afternoon, Barrett and I went out to fish the Colorado again. Our cabin is about seventy-five yards from the river. It is hard to imagine that seven hundred miles or so south of here this little creek of a river carves the Grand Canyon.

Barrett does all the fishing: I caddie the worms and tackle, which is enough for me. Sometimes I carry a book, but it usually is not as interesting as watching my son trying to catch a fish.

Yesterday was a bad day on the Colorado. Barrett tried his regular spot, which has been sweet every time, but yesterday he had no luck, not a strike. I suggested that we move upstream. We pushed through thick river willows and across fallen Lodge Pole pine, casting into every promising pool for over half a mile. Barrett moaned. If he goes without a catch for fifteen minutes, he declares that he never catches a fish. The day before he got seven Brookies out of the Colorado just below Never Summer Ranch, but by yesterday he had forgotten them.

We retreated downstream without a fish. After two hours, nothing. Barrett whined, so I reminded him that the best reason to fish is to learn the lessons fishing has to teach, like patience and how to put up with failure. But I suppose you have to fish for thirty or forty years before you can enjoy fishing when you are not catching fish. Barrett has been at it for only five or six years and can't comprehend being content just fishing, which is a matter, most of the time, of not catching fish.

It was after six o'clock when he said he wanted to try his favorite spot before we quit. To make good the time, I would sit in my chair and read *Lonesome Dove* to him. I have given up on getting my son to read proper great books, but now I have him hooked on Larry McMurtry. I don't know what he finds more interesting, the cowboys or the whores.

Barrett's two grandmothers wouldn't be happy if they knew I am letting their twelve-year old grandson read such a book. The cowboys would be okay, but not the whores. Grandmothers don't understand that you can't have one without the other.

Barrett laughed when Bert Borum says to Captain Call, "If you don't git me to a town soon I think I'm gonna marry a heifer." I paused on something Augustus says to Captain Call: "You're so sure you're right it doesn't matter to you whether people talk to you at all. I'm glad I've been wrong enough to keep in practice."

Captain Call objects: "Why would you want to keep in practice being wrong? I'd think it would be something you'd try to avoid."

But Augustus persists: "You can't avoid it, you've got to learn to handle it. If you only come face to face with your own mistakes once or twice in your life it's bound to be extra painful. I face mine every day—that way they ain't usually much worse than a dry shave."

I am more like Captain Call than Augustus: I never got used to being wrong. Maybe that's one reason I sometimes feel like I've lost everything when I think I've made a big mistake. I probably need to practice making mistakes. That way I wouldn't feel so bad when I make one—or I think I have.

About that time, Barrett said, "I got him." And he pulled up a nice little Brookie. "Go on," he said, "read some more," hooking a worm and casting back in. Sometimes I think I am working only to make my son happy.

I read on, getting to the place where Lippy tells the young cowboys that they need to be drunk when they go to the whores. Barrett's grandmothers would really be unhappy with me now. "You want to have plenty of alcohol in you," Lippy says, "before you slip up on one [of them whores]. Otherwise you'll start to take a leak some morning and your pecker will come right off in your hand."

To this startling prospect, Pete Spettle darkly replies, "Mine better not." Barrett chuckled enough to scare the fish. Then he shouted, "I got him," and he pulled in the biggest fish he has caught in the river yet, and his first Rainbow. Looking at the band of color glistening on his side, we saw why he is called Rainbow.

I read through three more fish and twenty more pages. Two bull elk crossed the river, not thirty feet away, and stopped to stare. I think they liked the reading. An otter swam across the stream. It was nearly dark.

"Dad," the young boy said, "this is my best day in Colorado yet, catching fish and reading *Lonesome Dove*." We walked to the cabin and he talked all the way.

So it happened to Barrett yesterday: he lost the day, but got it back. He got himself and Colorado back—me, too. By the time we reached the cabin, he was alive after birth.

If my friend Harry Kohler read all this stuff, he likely would say, "Well, Ted, sometimes you lose something and can't get it back."

Sometimes we do lose things and can't, or don't, get them back, things like our faith or a lover or a friend. The more common experience is to think that we won't get them back, when we will, or could. We may not be able to get everything back, but we can get something.

Fifteen years after he left Baylor, Hardy Jones decided one night that he had lost everything. I don't know whether he had his Christology worked out or not. Probably didn't. There Jones sat, as fine a teacher of ethics as one could hope to have, watching a *Bonanza* rerun one Sunday night in Lincoln, Nebraska. "I'm not going to put up with this anymore," he said to his friend, and Jones walked out the door, went to his office on the eleventh floor of the academic building at the University of Nebraska, opened the window, and jumped out.

Later I told Harry Kohler that Jones ought to have known that a man can't fly across Nebraska. I also suggested that, like a good Roman Stoic, Jones might have come to a considered decision to end his life, so we ought to respect his choice.

Harry felt about Jones just like he felt about those soldiers in Vietnam who let themselves get crotch rot: he was pissed off. "So Judy left him and took their kid to California," he said. "It wasn't the end of the world. It was narcissistic self-indulgence and self-pity, that's what it was."

Harry was probably right. I suspect everybody who knew Hardy kmew he was mistaken and tried to tell him. He might not have gotten everything back, but he might have recovered something.

"But, Estess," I can hear Kohler telling me, "you didn't respond to what I said. I asked about losing something you can't get back. You keep talking about thinking you have lost everything but later finding that you made a mistake. I'm talking about irrevocable loss, about losing something that is irreplaceable, something you can't get back."

Well, I tell you what: I feel a bit like Captain Call. I don't want to make a mistake here. So I tell you what I need to do. I need—I need to sleep on it.

But, for now, let me just say this: one morning when Sybil and Barrett and I were camping at Lake Granby, Sybil and Barrett were waiting for me in the car. Sybil noticed someone coming out of the john, and she said to Barrett: "Barrett, that old man looks a lot like Dad." And Barrett said, "Mom, that old man is Dad." Sybil and Barrett thought that was the funniest thing that happened all day.

It's true: I've lost my youth and can't get it back. That's an irrevocable loss. I wouldn't choose this loss if I had a choice; but it is unavoidable and irrevocable—because it is. It can't be undone. It's past. Indeed, from the beginning, losing my youth was a condition of having it at all.

As youths go, mine was a pretty good one. It was just given to me, so I ought at least to be grateful and not complain when it's gone. Losing my youth doesn't make me wish I never had it.

Sometimes that's the way it is with things we lose and can't get back. It hurts, but we willingly pay the price of losing them in order to have them as long as we do. We are grateful to have them, even at the certain cost of losing them. If we can't manage to be grateful, we usually turn out sad and disappointed, even bitter, which is not a wholesome way to be. It irritates other people and makes us unpleasant dinner guests.

Sybil and I sometimes imagine losing Barrett—irrevocably—and wonder whether we could manage, and how. We don't know, but we hope that we would not turn insufferably sad or bitter, but that, in time, we would come to say, "We are grateful to have had him, even at the cost of losing him. He was, after all, a gift."

We wouldn't love him any less because we lost him. Indeed, we would love him all the more.

# IV

Sybil's mother called this morning to report that Aunt Frances died in Bakersfield last night. Sybil and I talked about whether she would go out for the funeral. She once had four aunts in California. Now there are two.

It puts in mind when Sybil's last surviving great uncle died in Jasper County, Mississippi. Sybil wondered whether she ought to go to the funeral. At first, she decided not to; but I insisted; so she went. When she came back, she thanked me warmly. She said I was a thoughtful person, unselfish, and considerate. I was surprised.

Since such a small thing brought me to such pleasure in her sight, I now encourage Sybil to go to all the funerals I can. A funeral always does her, and me, some good. I look better to Sybil after she's been to a funeral, and these days my looks need all the help they can get.

But no, this time with Aunt Frances, Sybil would just call Uncle Earl. "Uncle Earl," she reported, "was glad I called. He said they were sitting at the dinner table when Aunt Frances just fell over. Must have been a heart attack. He said she was ready to die. She couldn't drive anymore, and couldn't keep up with her money, and couldn't remember yesterday. He said it was like she was living some place else. He wanted to know if Barrett is catching any fish. You remember, Uncle Earl loves to fish."

Ted L. Estess

Earl lost Frances and won't get her back. That's the kind of loss I don't have much to say about. I don't have much experience losing things I can't get back, unless you count my youth.

Elizabeth Bishop, who is Sybil's favorite poet, has something to say about all this in a poem called "One Art." The "art" Bishop is talking about is the art of losing. Oddly, four times in the short poem, we read, "The art of losing isn't hard to master." She mentions a crescendo of losses over the course of her life, disparate things such as keys and "hours badly spent" and her mother's watch and "three loved houses" and places where she has lived. Given the ubiquity of loss, the poem counsels that one should "practice losing farther, losing faster" so as to master the art of losing. In an ascending scale of losses, the poem arrives finally to focus on the most grievous loss of all:

> Even losing you (the joking voice, a gesture
> I love) I shan't have lied. It's evident
> the art of losing's not too hard to master
> though it may look like (*Write* it!) like disaster.

We shouldn't miss the irony of Bishop's poem. Such irony with regard to one's losses—such loving detachment, such practiced letting go—is hard to achieve, hard to master.

Insofar as possible, the poet masters irrevocable loss by turning it into words. That's what she means when she says, "*Write* it!" Writing does not bring back what she loved and lost, but writing places and shapes and corrals the loss. More important, writing helps her more fully love what she lost. Deepened by loss, love has a way of righting her life, insofar as it can be righted.

Loss is hard to master, if for no other reason than that it is hard to be a poet of one's own life. It is hard to turn life and loss into words, much less into poetry. It is easier to let loss remain as undifferentiated, unshaped, emotional stuff. But that seems to be what loss requires of us if it is not to be only a disaster: we have to turn it into words, to write, or at least talk about it. The person who is a poet of her own life takes loss—but not only loss—and makes something of it.

Perhaps writing, then, is a way of *righting* the loss. When so shaped and placed and corralled by words, loss becomes what it is—a part, not the whole of life. Life thus is righted, not in the sense that one would ever say that the loss was right or good. It is, after all, loss. Like I said before, one wouldn't choose the loss if one had a choice; but it is unavoidable and irrevocable—because it is. It is done. It is past.

Writing is a way of righting the loss in the sense that a ship is righted in heavy seas. It is a way of recovering balance, equilibrium, so that one may go on. It's strange, but perhaps true: against the storm of loss, words can be the ballast of one's life. It's not much, but it is something.

Writing loss, then, is a way of putting things into perspective, not into any old perspective, but into a perspective that deepens love precisely as it deepens one's sense of loss. Such love—love that is deepened by the loss, actual or imagined, of things you can't get back—sometimes has a way of making one's life seem more nearly right.

## A Fishing Medley
### I

For a month now, twelve-year-old Barrett has lusted after the big fish in the lake. He tried catching them a month ago when we first arrived, but had no luck. So he quit the lake and went to the river where bringing home a few Brookies is almost a sure thing.

But to my surprise, yesterday morning Barrett decided to go after the big fish again. This time he would use something called power bait, which is designed to work on fish like Brut is supposed to work on women: they fall irresistibly under its spell, enchanted, bedazzled, and doomed. The difference is that power bait stinks.

Barrrett baited and waited, and like Brut, his new strategy worked: he hooked one, the big one, the really big one. Rarely does one have the opportunity to witness such a concentration of desire and hankering for greatness as I did watching Master Barrett struggle with that fish. This would be his story to tell, he knew it; but with the trophy three feet from shore the line snapped, and Leviathan swam free.

Anguish and anger mastered Master Barrett. Throwing down his rod and breaking its tip were the least of it. I told Barrett that he will catch another fish, but he was beyond consolation.

"*Daaaddd*," he asserted, "I'll never catch another fish as big as that one. You know that."

"No, son," I said, "I don't know that."

By evening the youngster decided to try again. This time, he would stake his line in the water overnight. It is low order fishing, but frustrated anglers will sink to any level to land a prize. And on this very morning at 7:18 a.m., Master Barrett pulled in a beautiful fish, surely not as big as the one that got away, but a fish correspondent with his sense of himself—big.

This evening, then, it's understandable that the boy is eager to try again. Walking down to the lake, I suggest, "Barrett, put this line in the lake close to the cabin, and we'll put the other one down the way." I am surprised when he takes my advice and casts out.

On the way back to the cabin after setting the second line, Barrett says, "Dad, wouldn't it be great if I've already caught a fish."

"Stranger things have happened," I say. We arrive at the first line just in time to see the bobber disappear.

Judging from the bend in the rod, we both know it is a big one. I know Barrett fears a repetition of the day before, but he calculates, alternates strategies, lets the fish run, and reels in, keeping the tension and tiring the fish. I'm puzzled to see that the boy knows so well what to do with a big fish, and wonder how he learned all this, not from me, that's for sure. Suddenly the fish throws its entire body up into the dim light of dusk. "Barrett," I yell, "he's *huugggee.*"

"Dad, get the net, get the net." The battle at the pitch, I run to the cabin; but returning with the net, I hear in the gathering darkness a voice quiet and filled with sadness so infinite that it could move angels to weep. "Dad, he got away."

No, I think, this is too much for any Barrett to bear. Are we brought into this bitter world only for such as this? Better not to fish at all than repeatedly to sink beneath such disappointment.

Suddenly he shouts, "*Daaaddd.* He's still on." The darkness lifts, and the struggle of boy with fish resumes.

Somewhere Wallace Stevens says, "Perhaps the truth depends upon a walk around a lake."

For these ten or so minutes, truth for Master Barrett depends alone on the struggle to get that big one from the lake. Truth here is not the truth of syllogisms or empirical demonstrations or factual statements. Truth here is something that happens. It is the moment when one's very self is uncovered, displayed, when the inclinations and possibilities of one's self coincide with the possibility present before one. In this moment one comes to know oneself by connecting with, or by meeting someone or something that is decidedly not one's self, in Barrett's case, a fish. The day before, the truth of the boy depended on the one that got away. This evening it depends on the struggle again to land the really big one. And, he does.

# Fishing Spirit Lake

The fish in the net, the boy is ecstatic, out of breath and complete in himself. He hugs his father, and we walk hand-in-hand back to the cabin, he carrying the fish, I the rod. The boy is as tall as the mountain and wide as the evening sky.

I am inside the cabin getting the camera and the tape measure with which to document the catch when I hear from the deck, "Dad! You won't believe it. You won't believe it."

Even when I see for myself, I don't believe it. "Don't you see?" he asks. "This is the same fish. I caught the one that got away."

Things like this don't happen, at least not to people I know; but, indeed, Barrett's hook from the day before is in the fish's lip, there's no doubt about it. He did not catch a fish *like* the one that got away: he caught the very fish. Yesterday he thought that managing disappointment was tough. This evening, his astonishment is even more boggling to the imagination. How can he get his thoughts and feelings, mind and heart, around this mysterious, inexplicable, capricious superfluity of goodness.

So the boy caught two big fish on a single day, one in the morning and one in the evening. In the evening he got back what he had lost the day before. Disappointment forgotten, he goes to bed, his fragile faith renewed that the world, on balance, is good, open and full of possibilities, at least some of the time. But the question remains, will young Barrett bear it? Will he enter into, undergo deeply, a world so brindled with disappointment and satisfaction?

# II

"One more, Dad, just one more." Were it not the fourth time that he has said this, I might believe him. Surely all boys are not this way: some must listen to their fathers when they complain of its getting dark and being too cold to fish.

"Barrett," I protest, "I can barely see, and I'm freezing."

"Dad, the fishing's too good to leave now, just one more."

We've been at this for almost four hours now. When the two of us left the cabin, the sun was still thirty degrees high. The Colorado River here in the National Park still sparkled in the sunlight when Barrett threw in his line for the first time. It was over an hour before the shadows of the

Ted L. Estess

Never Summer Mountains that rise from the valley floor less than a half mile to the west of us began to fall over the river and yet another two hours beyond that before the shadows dissipated into darkness. Now, even at 9:15 p.m. the latter process is not complete. So he and I—at least at close range—are still visible to one another. His young eyes can still make out the river willows, at least the silhouettes, hanging over the river. His method of fishing allows him to continue, as well. It's primitive.

When we started, I suggested that Barrett try this way of fishing in a shallow, rapidly flowing river stream that has only an occasional pool. It is something that my college roommate Jerry Brown taught me when we went fishing for a few days in the summer of 1962 in the mountains of Southwest Colorado. Since Barrett is only twelve years old, it's still legal for him to fish this way in the Rocky Mountain National Park. He simply throws the rig—which consists of a quarter-ounce piece of lead and a small hook baited with a night crawler—into the stream and lets it follow the flow of the water, bouncing among the rocks as it goes. As I said, it is primitive way to fish.

Before throwing this rig into the Colorado for the first time, he says, "I'm not going to catch any fish this way." He has already had luck with night crawlers in the Colorado near our cabin, but he is fishing in deep pools there.

"Jerry Brown and I caught lots of fish this way."

"I tell you what, Dad, I bet you an ice cream cone that I don't catch anything in three casts this way."

"Okay," I say, "I'll take that bet." I observe that my son has a strange way of betting. He bets against what he really wants to happen. He wants to catch a fish, so he bets an ice cream cone that he will not. It is a way, I suppose, of hedging the bet that any fisherman makes whenever he cast out a rig, regardless of the level of sophistication. The casting out is itself something of a bet. What differentiates fisherman from one another is that the better fishermen know how to improve the odds. Barrett figures, I surmise, that if he catches a fish on one of his first three casts, he will have won what's most important to him even at the cost of a cone at the Dairy Bar in Grand Lake. If he doesn't catch a fish, he will lose the bet, yet still win an ice cream cone. Pretty clever, I think.

So he throws the rig into the Colorado and allows it to float downstream toward the Brookies who are always there, facing upstream, their brown speckled bodies camouflaged against the variegated rocks below, waiting for something to come their way. In less than a minute, I say, "It's looks like I'm going to have an ice cream cone at the Dairy Bar tomorrow."

Later I tell Barrett that I should have doubled-down on every cast. After I explain what "double-down" means, I tell him that had I done so I would be eating ice cream cones for the rest of the summer, so many Brookies he has caught this afternoon. No wonder the boy says, even after nearly four hours, "One more fish, Dad, just one more."

"And, Dad, remember that we spent more than thirty minutes looking at the elk. That took time away from fishing."

Indeed, we did. At about 7 p.m., Barrett had said, "Dad, look there." And he pointed south down into the meadow that spreads west of the river and beneath the mountains of Never Summer.

"That's something, Barrett. Let's go get a better look." And he, without complaint, reeled in his line. We pushed through the thick river willows and walked up to the gravel trail and stepped into the meadow on the other side and started walking slowly to the south.

"How many are there, Dad?"

"A lot," I said. "Let's go a little closer and count. Remember the ranger said not to get too close."

We stopped counting at a hundred-and-thirty. More than one-hundred-and-thirty bull elk, that's what we saw, bull elk of all ages and sizes, some yearlings, some four and five-year olds, some grand, magnificent elder ones, whose racks seemed much too large for them to carry. I wondered if these grand ones would make it through one more rutting season, one more winter. It left Barrett and me speechless; and rightly so, for we saw something that very few people get to see if for no other reason than that bull elk, at least that many, seldom congregate.

"But it was worth it," he adds, as if to let me know that he realizes that fishing is not the only thing his father is interested in. At about that time, he feels the tugs on the line and starts reeling in another Brookie.

"One more, Dad, just one more," he says.

I think to myself, "That's the way it is with fisherman: give them two fish, they want three; give them three, they want four; *ad infinitum*. No wonder that the Game and Fish Commission sets limits. I wonder if this boy of mine will ever be satisfied.

## III

He has thought about it for a couple of years. His grandfather—Sybil's step-father, "Racehorse" Cochran—even gave him a fly rod for Christmas two years ago, but he wasn't ready for it. The rod sat at the house until last week when we were packing to come up here to Colorado. He said he would like to take it along just in case. I called myself being careful, but I broke the tip getting the rod in the trunk of the car. Barrett was magnanimous, but magnanimity comes cheap to him. "That's okay," Dad, he said, "we can get another one."

So after lunch, we drive fifteen miles south to Granby to get Barrett set up for fly fishing. Driving down, I think how strange it is for me to give this much time to fishing. I never fished at all before Barrett, except for a few days with Jerry Brown in 1962 and another half dozen days in Montana in 1975. And here I am spending the best part of Barrett's youth and my middle years helping him catch fish. Today I am giving another Colorado afternoon driving fifteen miles to pay a hundred bucks for a fly rod in which I have little or no interest.

"Dad," Barrett interrupts to say, "where do you think we should try first with the fly rod?" I notice that in talking of fishing he always uses the plural first-person pronoun "we," and wonder if he has a frog in his pocket.

"Oh, I think that we might try the canal that links Granby and Shadow Mountain lakes where we were the other night. You'll need plenty of room getting started."

For years parents have been told that they are the determinative influence on the way their children turn out. All the books on parenting tell you that. Read books to the child, and the child will be a reader. Introduce good music into the child's environment, and the child will be musical and like good music. Promote neatness and order in the house, and the child will be neat and orderly. Even the Good Book promotes this notion: "Bring up a child in the way that he should go, and when he is old, he will not depart from it." It sounds simple enough: makes parenting sound something like climbing a mountain.

As we pass Shadow Mountain Lake, it occurs to me: I don't believe it, not any more. Often these days I don't see a connection between how parents parent and the way their children turn out. Sybil's and my experience with this boy is sufficient evidence, but take Christine and Christopher, the two children of good friends of ours. Christine is in Bonn, an assistant to the chair of the foreign relations committee of the *Bundestag*. To hear her parents tell it, she is in charge of German foreign relations, two years out of college. After quitting high school, her brother Christopher is a short-order cook in Midland, trying to stay clean. The parents did the same thing, or close to it, with both kids. Should they take credit for one kid, who is helping run the world, and blame for the other, who is as lost as a rabbit in Grand Central Station? I've already told Barrett I don't want any credit for what he does in this world, just so I don't have to take the blame. He can credit and blame himself.

"Dad, I can't stand that music," Barrett complains in response to the tape that I have playing in the car. "Who is that? Beethoven again?"

We come to the end of Lake Granby, and I know I'm right. There is positive discontinuity between my parenting and the way he's turning out. There's no connection between him and me. When I was his age, I loved Beethoven. I wanted to study piano so I could play the *Appassionata Sonata*. I didn't know anything more beautiful than the second movement, beautiful because of its reserve, its simplicity and profundity. Today I'm riding to Granby to buy a fly rod for a thirteen-year old teenager I barely know. This stranger sitting with me in the car, he's just hitching a ride and bumming money off me.

Even the fishing, it was Sybil's mother who got Barrett caught on that. I didn't do it. Sybil's mother thinks a body has nothing better to do than get to some water in Mississippi with a can of worms or a bucket of minnows and catch a few small-mouth bass before dark. "Marion," I tell her, "you've about ruint that boy of mine. He's never going to mount to much of anything if he keeps on fishing all the time." But she always replies, "Fishing is mountin' to something."

And this crazy idea of fly fishing, it's Marion and her husband Racehorse's fault. One afternoon at Magnolia Lake in South Mississippi when Barrett was eight or nine years old, he was out fishing with Marion and Racehorse. In less than thirty minutes Racehorse had two dozen bream in the cooler. Barrett was caught not by the idea of it, but by the thing itself. And that thing was fishing.

But it's clear what I'm going to do: I'm going to help this boy fish as long as he will let me. Without him, I would never wet a line; but with him, I will buy the pole and sit beside the river as long as I can. I might even take a cassette along and play Brahms as I read and watch. Maybe he could learn to love the Brahms *Intermezzos* and feel the yearning of those old melodies. Or perhaps I could hook him on *David Copperfield*, not the magician but the novel, as I was when I was in the eighth grade.

He will have none of it, I know. I might as well give it up. Let go. But I'm like Henry Bech, that character of Updike, who says that he's "bad at the business of life, which is letting go." Is that indeed the business of life? Letting go?

But that's what I've got to do: let go. Get unhooked from the picture that is holding me captive. It's a picture of me, of what I was and what I wish I were. That's the picture I cast onto Barrett. It's the bait I try to catch him with. But one me is enough. Better one good Barrett than another shadowy reflection of me. Better his reality than my fantasy.

On the way back from Granby we listen to *Guns and Roses*. I can't understand a word they sing, if you call what they sing "words" and what they are doing "singing." In the back seat lies the fly rod we bought at Bill's Tackle store. Of course, I had to buy a case for it, too. But I have to admit the rod is a beauty, made by a man who lives in the foothills nine miles west of town, out toward Hot Sulphur Springs. When we asked about buying a fly rod, Bill called him and the man drove in with it while we waited in the store. As he passed the rod into Barrett's hands, he quietly said, "I made this rod, son, and you take good care of it. And remember, fly fishing is a good way to catch fish, but don't give up on other ways. That's the worst thing fly fishermen do. They think fly fishing is the only way to fish. It's not." Turning to Bill, he added, "That right, Bill?" Bill said, "That's right." Bill ought to know: he holds the record catch of a trout from some lake down in Arizona, and he didn't catch that fish with a fly rod either.

On the way home Barrett and I stop at the canal linking the two lakes to try the new rod. It's a fine one. He's frustrated but persistent, and it's clear that he will get the hang of it with practice. It makes me think that maybe I'll take that rod I broke down to Granby next week. The man who made Barrett's said he could repair it. That's what I'll do: have that man put a new tip on that rod and give it a try.

## IV

Before my son drafted me to caddy his tackle box alongside the rivers and lakes of Colorado, I had never paid much attention to the way we use metaphors drawn from fishing with which to probe the density of meaning that resides in other human activities. That's part, I think, of the power of fishing: it offers rich metaphoric possibilities. Take, for instance, the way in which people pull language from fishing to speak of the mystery that resides in the coming together of a lover and a beloved. "She's quite a catch," that's what several people told me when Sybil and I got together. Another said, "Man, you fell for her, hook, line, and sinker." Sybil tells me that one of her friends teased her by saying, "You're going to feel mighty bad if you don't land that guy." When things don't work out between two people, you hear, "Too bad, she got away. But, remember, there are other fish in the lake."

The implication in all these expressions is that one uses one's self, or some aspect of one's self, as bait with which to catch a prize. Present yourself—as a fly fisherman presents a fly to the fish—in the right way to the one you are trying to catch and you will be irresistible.

But this is a rough analogy between fishing and the way potential lovers relate to one another. Such talk is something to be used by ad agents. To the skilled fishermen, who can be as subtle as heart surgeons, it misses both the richness of their passion for, and the complexity of fishing. It also misses whatever it is that draws two persons together.

In a genuine meeting, there is, first, the casting out and into, and seeing what comes up from, the depths. As when you are standing on the side of a lake fishing, you stand at the edge of a person, anticipating, present to something you can't fully see. You don't even know if what you long for and very much need is there. You have a hunch, an inclination, an apprehension before the fact, but it is only a hunch. When you cast out, you, as it were, cast yourself out. You cast yourself forward to an unknown possibility, an unknown truth. At the outset, the truth that can happen between two persons is unknown, precisely because it has not happened yet.

Perhaps what you seek is there, awaiting you, perhaps it's not. But even if it is, it is in the depths where you can't see. If things go right, a moment comes when you feel a pull on the line. You connect across the distance with something that is not yourself. Your entire self comes awake with anticipation and some apprehension. What you desire may break loose or snap the line. You may fail fully to connect.

All the time you are present, *there*, expecting. Perhaps, just perhaps, that which you need and very much want is already coming to meet you. When—or if—it arrives, it is still a surprise, even though you've been waiting for it a long time. For you never know what is hidden in the depths. You never know, beforehand, what will surface. Strange, impossible things emerge from the depths all the time.

And the process is reciprocal: while you are anticipating and awaiting, you are being anticipated and awaited. You are both fisherman and fish, both lover and beloved, both relating and being related to. You present yourself to one who presents herself to you. You are present, presenting, and being presented to. You are a present, a gift, and you receive one as well. It is a delightful process, complex too, at the same time to be both in the light on the bank and in the dark of the depths.

When connection happens, grace abounds.

## Becoming Part of a Story
## I

Late in the day Barrett and I row down to the deep water at the end of Sun Valley Lake. He wants to try a new lure called a *Mepps*. To his amazement, the Mepps no more than touches the water when a big Rainbow hits it.

We move around the lake for a couple more hours and Barrett tosses that Mepps out another two hundred times, but he never gets another strike. He is puzzled. How is it that he catches a trout on the first cast and never touches another the rest of the day?

To a considerable extent, it is a fortuitous matter, catching a fish. The fisherman only helps good fortune along; he wants at least not to get in the way. Some folks can't stand that about fishing, so they give it up.

All this reminds me of the series of events that led me to Houston, Texas, three decades ago. It began when my phone rang in Missoula, Montana. The voice said, "This is Donald Lutz from the University of Houston." I had never heard of Lutz, never thought of the University of Houston.

"I'm calling to invite you to be a consultant for us. Gerald Hinkle recommended you."

I started to ask, "What's a consultant?" And I didn't tell Lutz I wouldn't have known Gerald Hinkle if he walked in the door.

Later I recalled meeting Hinkle at a conference in Williamsburg, Virginia. We ended up going out to dinner together. I wanted to try the peanut soup at Aunt Sally's Tavern.

I've met lots of people at lots of meetings, but this one time in Virginia I meet Hinkle; and two years later Hinkle meets Lutz at a meeting in Arkansas; and then a year after that Lutz calls me in Montana, thereby setting in motion a series of events that led to my moving to Texas. My intersecting Hinkle in Virginia and then his intersecting Lutz in Arkansas were at least as improbable as the first cast of Barrett's Mepps landing right on top of that trout in the deep water of Sun Valley Lake.

Had I decided to eat a hamburger alone at Wendy's instead of going with Hinkle for some of that god-awful peanut soup at Aunt Sally's Tavern, my life in Houston, Texas, never would have happened. Thirty-one years of life in Houston would have been . . . well, it would have been nothing. Not a thing.

Now some one might say, "That's just the way life is, Estess. What's the big deal?"

Well, to Estess, it is a big deal. It's my life I'm talking about, and I don't like thinking that my life, *as I have lived it*, may never have been. If it may never have been, it somehow seems flimsy, shadowy, inconsequential. I've heard that song about life being but a vapor in mid-summer's day and all that, but somehow I want my life to be more substantial, more solid. If it's not, the game doesn't seem worth the candle, and why am I spending all this time thinking about it?

A book arrived in yesterday's mail, a gift from my friend John Smith. The inscription says: "Ted & Barrett, drop everything & read this book. John." I tend to do what I am told, so last night I started reading *All the Pretty Horses* by Cormac McCarthy and came quickly to like John Grady Cole and Lacey Rawlins, two young cowboys living around San Angelo, Texas. One night John Grady and Rawlins lie down on a blacktop road to watch the stars:

> Rawlins propped the heel of one boot atop the top of the other. As if to pace off the heavens. My daddy run off from home when he was fifteen. Otherwise I'd of been born in Alabama.
> You wouldnt of been born at all.
> Whut makes you say that?
> Cause your mama's from San Angelo and he never would of met her.
> He'd of met somebody.
> So would she.
> So?
> So you wouldnt of been born.
> I dont see why you say that. Ida of been born somewheres.

# Fishing Spirit Lake

How?

Well why not?

If your mama had a baby with her other husband and your daddy had one with his other wife which one would you be?

I wouldn't be nether one of em.

That's right.

Rawlins lay watching the stars. After a while he said: I could still be born. I might look different or somethin. If God wanted me to be born I'd be born.

And if He didn't you wouldnt.

You're makin my goddamn head hurt.

Some years ago, I made my goddamn head hurt trying to get through a big book by Jean Paul Sartre called *Being and Nothingness*. Like most folks who tried, I never made it, but I caught the drift. Sartre uses the French words *de trop* to capture something of what John Grady Cole is talking about. An occurrence—like Lacey Rawlins' getting born in Texas—is *de trop* if it has this accidental, fortuitous quality about it. "Contingent" is another word philosophers use to talk about the same thing. An occurrence is contingent if it may just as well have happened as not. An occurrence—indeed, a life—that depends so thoroughly on the unlikely intersection of Estess and Hinkle in Aunt Sally's Tavern and on the subsequent intersection of Hinke and Lutz in Arkansas is thoroughly contingent. It is *de trop*. Thinking about that makes my goddamn head hurt.

Now some folks are different from me. When they see how chancy life is, they're ready to have a go at it. They enjoy taking chances as long as they have a chance to take chances.

Others are like Sartre. They try to face up to the contingency and even to the absurdity of their choices—like my choosing to try the peanut soup at Aunt Sally's Tavern.

But for the life of me, I've never been able to respond like that, and I tell you why: I wasn't reared that way. It's in the rearing, that's what it is.

Now philosophers may scoff at this, but it's the only refutation—if I may use the word—to Sartre I've ever come up with. When he says that my life—thoroughly contingent because it is so thoroughly dependent upon the improbable intersection of Estess and Hinkle at Aunt Sally's tavern and then of Hinkle and Lutz in Arkansas—is as insubstantial as vapor floating off a lake, then I just have to say: I wasn't reared that way.

But I have to confess that my life felt mighty vaporous, mighty *de troppy* in the long months after I moved to Texas. I felt that I may as well be—or not be—somewhere else. It was as though I was somewhere I wasn't supposed to be, living a life I wasn't supposed to be living.

"That's why," I said to Michael one day, "I feel so bad." Michael was a therapist-friend who helped me out quite a bit during those first months.

"What's why?" Michael asked.

"Why I feel so bad moving to Houston."

"Last week you told me you didn't think you would ever figure it out, and here you are this week still trying to figure it out."

"That was last week," I said.

"Well?"

"I feel bad because it's all an accident, my even being in Houston, Texas. It may just as well not have happened. None of it."

"That's curious," he said, and he started laughing. I don't know why, but his laughing got me to giggling, too. Before I had a chance to say anything, Michael said, "Our time is up for today. But, Ted, there's another possibility."

"What's that?" I asked.

"Instead of feeling bad you could feel good."

I said, "I doubt it."

## II

Out here in Colorado this summer I've taken to rereading some old books. Barrett just finished reading *A River Runs Through It* for the third time, so I decided to take up Norman Maclean's fine book myself. I know it's only a coincidence and strange to say, but my friend John Smith sent this book to me fifteen years ago, and here this week he sends me another. Norman Maclean talks about growing up in Missoula, Montana:

> By the middle of that summer when I was seventeen I had yet to see myself become part of a story. I had as yet no notion that life every now and then becomes literature—not for long, of course,

but long enough to be what we best remember, and often enough so that what we eventually come to mean by life are those moments when life, instead of going sideways, backwards, forward, or nowhere at all, lines out straight, tense and inevitable, with a complication, climax, and, given some luck, a purgation, as if life had been made and not [just] happened.

To tell the truth, that's the way I was reared to think of life. The Baptists did it to me. From the time I was knee high to a grasshopper, good-hearted preachers and widow women told me that Good God Almighty had nothing better to do than make a plan for my life. I thus came to expect my life to line out straight, tense, and inevitable and for all the parts of it to go together like parts of a well-made story.

At the same time, other good folks were saying, "Young, man, you can do anything you want to do, be anything you want to be." In other words, I was to make up my life. But while I was trying to make it up, it felt like my life was going sideways, backwards, forwards, or nowhere at all.

Now this is a strange, even contradictory situation to be in: to be hearing, on the one hand, that somehow your life is planned even before you begin living it, and, on the other, to be hearing that your life is up for grabs. The first places you before one great Necessity; the other places you before an infinite number of possibilities.

To some extent what the Baptists said about life made me feel pretty good. After all, it was rather invigorating to think that Good God Almighty had a plan for little old Teddy Lynn Estess way down there in little old Tylertown, Mississippi. That view made things pretty simple: all you have to do is figure out the plan and get on it.

The problem arose, of course, in the middle of life, when I saw that something so momentous as moving to the fair city of Houston, Texas, turned on so fragile a matter as a cup of peanut soup. I didn't seem to be living a life that had been made by any Great Maker or Planner of all of life.

Nor did I seem to be living a life of my own making. It wasn't clear what story, if any, I was in; but it was clear that whatever was happening wasn't altogether of my own making. It was as though my life was being constructed out of fortuitous happenings and tortured choices, happenings and choices that could just as well have been otherwise or not been at all. Mine seemed a tenuous little life with no foundation at all.

"Michael," I said the next week, "I feel like I'm walking on thin air."

"That's the way I felt when I decided not to be a priest anymore."

"What?" I said. "You were a priest? I didn't know that."

"For eighteen years. I taught theology at a seminary for a while. Even studied in Rome."

"Then you know what I'm talking about."

"Maybe," he said. "Maybe you feel like you're walking on thin air because of a discrepancy. It's the discrepancy between a picture you have of life and the life you're living."

"How's that?"

"Well, the life you are living seems more fluid, risky and chancy than your picture of life allows, that's all. It's a common thing. Just change your picture of life and you remove the discrepancy. Maybe then you wouldn't feel so bad."

"But, Michael," I said, "don't you think there's something to what the Baptists said about—"

"Ted," he said, "I'm sorry to interrupt, but our time is up."

What I was getting ready to say when Michael called time on me was that maybe the old Baptist widow women weren't complete idiots in suggesting that one might live life as though it is made, and before made, planned. Maybe one can see one's life that way. And wouldn't it be something to have both things at once: at the same time to acknowledge the fluidity and contingency in one's life, even to enjoy that, and to have the solidity and firmness that come from living a life that, in some sense, is made, where all the parts seem to fit.

"Michael," I said the next week, "I want both."

"Both what?"

"I want the old picture I had of life and to be truthful about feeling that my life turns on chance."

"That's curious," he said. "I thought we decided last week that the discrepancy is painful. To remove the pain you have to remove the discrepancy, which means you have to give up that old picture of life of your life being planned before you live it. You just have to give that up."

I said, "I don't want to give that up."

"That's not surprising," he said. "You were reared that way. Still . . . ."

And here Michael's sentence trailed off and silence took over for a while. After a minute or two of silence, I asked, "Well," I said, "what are you thinking?"

"It's a possibility," he said.

"Really?"

"Really. But I still think you're making a mistake."

"What's that?"

"You want prospectively what you can only have retrospectively."

I wasn't sure I was understanding a thing the man was saying, so it made sense to ask, "What are you saying?"

"Just what I said," he said. "I mean that retrospectively—when you are looking back—life can acquire the kind of stability and firmness your old picture promised you. The story of your life can acquire a degree of stability and firmness, but I think you may have to wait a while for it."

"Wait for what?" I asked.

"Wait to have a deep-down sense that your life could have been no other way."

"But you said I'm making a mistake. What's the mistake?"

"It's what I said. The mistake is to expect prospectively what you can only have retrospectively. Prospectively, your life will continue to be fluid, chancy."

"That's bad," I said.

"There's another possibility."

I said, "I doubt it."

"You may find it interesting or fun. You would have to practice, but you may."

"May what?"

"May find the chanciness of life interesting or just plain fun."

I said, "I doubt it."

"Like I said, you would have to practice a long time."

"But," I asked, "what about that old Baptist picture?"

"That's not just Baptist, you know," Michael said. And then he took off talking about St. Augustine's *Confessions*. I almost interrupted to tell him that I was paying to talk to him not to listen to him talk to me. He went on to say that when Saint Augustine was forty-five or so, he wrote about how he got to be who he was. By that point his life had acquired a kind of inevitability about it. That's what gave him authority as a teacher. He felt as though his life could have been no other way, that his life was as it was from the very beginning.

I wanted to say, "That's what I want, Michael, and what I don't have and don't expect to have." But I didn't.

Then Michael said, "Whenever I taught Augustine to the seminarians, I asked them to memorize one line from *The Confessions*. The line goes like this: "sic curas unumquemque nostrum tamquam solum cures, et sic omnes tamquam singulos."

"Michael," I said, "Baptists don't do Latin."

"Oh," he said, "I forgot." Then he started talking again, this time explaining that when Augustine wrote that line he was at a sufficient remove from certain events of his life that he could see how things fit together, and that the line is speaking of Augustine's sense of providential care in all things of his life.

"Michael," I said, "what does the Latin mean?"

"Oh," he said, "it means, 'He cares for every one of us as though he had no other for whom to care. He cares for all as he cares for each.'"

"That's curious."

"Yes," he said, "it is."

Over the years I've thought a good deal about what my friend said that day. In many ways, he was right: I was making a mistake. I sometimes still make it. The mistake is to expect always to feel that life is unfolding as it ought to unfold, as it has to unfold. To want too quickly for the pieces of life to cohere as in a well-wrought story.

I've tried to give it up, but I sometimes catch myself making the same mistake. Only now, I don't call it a mistake. I call it "my way of getting on."

When you get past fifty years old—and maybe before—you may at times see a pattern in life and see life lining out straight, tense, and inevitable. You may see your life becoming part of a story. And the story of your life may seem so stable that it feels as though it might well have been made in advance of your living it. Even those things that presented themselves as so much sand blowing in the wind may seem, retrospectively, somehow inevitable. Without them you would have missed part of the story and every part somehow seems necessary for the whole life to be what it is. At some point, somehow the parts seem mysteriously to fit together and form a whole grander and more satisfying than anything you ever could have imagined.

But once you get past fifty or sixty years old, you've had world and time enough to see why Saint Augustine would confess "the soul is a great abyss," even as he discerns providential care at every step. This great explorer of the great abyss, then, fesses up to a deep-down and abiding ignorance about himself. Only in the shadow of a confession of abysmal ignorance about the deepest things of himself could he—or my friend Michael, or anyone, for that matter—venture something so audacious, something so comically exuberant, as "He cares for everyone of us as though he had no other for whom to care. He cares for all as he cares for each."

# The Point of Fishing
## I

"He left it for you to carry, didn't he?" That's what the lady at the counter of Shadow Mountain Lake Marina says to me as my fifteen-year old son Barrett walks out the door.

"Yep," I say, "I buy and carry."

"My kids do the same thing," she says. "They're all alike. You can't teach 'em anything."

"I'm still trying," I say. I tuck away the VISA card, and gather up two soda pops, three lures called rooster tails, a pack of crackers, a Snickers bar, and my daypack.

"Hope you have better luck fishing," she says. "Catch you later." I step into the sunshine, barely able to open the door for all the stuff I'm carrying.

"Dad, this boat is a piece of crap, and you know it," Barrett says, as he eases us away from the dock. I had asked him whether he might get a professional discount on the boat rental, working as he does this summer as a boat-jockey at Grand Lake Marina, just up the road from Shadow Mountain Lake. Our seventeen-foot run-about has a thirty-horsepower Mercury outboard, but Barrett is right: it's a piece of crap. Still, I'm the one who forked over fifty bucks to rent the thing. The least he can do is not complain.

"I'm not complaining, Dad, really, I'm not," he adds, without my saying anything. He knows me well enough to catch what I'm thinking. "Wow," he says. "Look at that." And he eyes a twenty-one foot Bayliner, blue and white, with a 110-horsepower Evinrude, passing by.

"Boats don't catch fish," I say. "People catch fish."

"Dad, you've said that a thousand times. Will you get off it?"

The day is pristine, about sixty-five degrees, with a high blue sky and a scattering of marshmallow clouds. Back in the cabin, Sybil is happy, writing poems. In a boat on Shadow Mountain Lake, Barrett is happy, setting out to fish. Though gray and paunchy, I guess I ought to be happy, too, in a boat, with my son and water, mountains and sky, light and air. What could be finer than to be in Colorado in the morning?

Somewhere Philip Roth says, "After the crack-up comes the grateful rush into ordinary life." I've had enough crack-ups to know what the man is talking about.

Captain Barrett is in charge, that much is clear no sooner than we cast off. "I drive until we start trolling," he says.

"Yessir, Captain," I say, settling into the seat, willing to be told what to do for the rest of the morning.

"Okay, Dad, you tie a rooster tail on that line," the fifteen-year old Captain directs, as he brings the boat to a halt.

"Yessir."

"Now, Dad, you handle the boat and take us slowly through the channel while I get these lines out."

"Yessir, Captain, whatever you say."

"Dad, a little slower."

"Yessir."

"That's too slow, Dad. The lines are getting too deep."

"Yessir."

"Too fast, Dad. Slower."

"Yessir."

"Dad, can't you keep it at the same speed? And will you stop calling me Captain."

"Yessir," and so it goes through the first hour, with the pattern interrupted only by the one fish we are to catch all morning long.

Finally, Barrett asks, "What are we doing wrong, Dad?"

"We aren't doing anything wrong, son."

"But we aren't catching any fish."

"How many times do I have to tell you there are other things to fishing than catching fish."

"How many times do I have to tell you that's crazy?"

"It might be crazy, but I think you can enjoy fishing whether you catch fish or not. You remember what the Park Ranger told us a couple of years ago, don't you?"

"Dad, you've said it thousand times." In his sing-songy voice, he mocks me by saying, "Every day is a good day for fishing, but not every day is a good day for catching fish." I am tempted to appeal to the beauty of the snowcapped Indian Peaks out across the bow and to the impressive vista of Shadow Mountain off to port as sufficient justification for being on the lake this morning. But that would be futile: the boy is unmoved by beauty.

I am almost at the point of calling attention to the pleasure of son and father being together, but I know that would be cause for greater scoffing yet. I don't need derision from my only son. Inexplicably, I try again.

"Son, I think the ranger was right. You've got to learn to enjoy fishing when you're not catching fish, because, most times, that's what fishing is, not catching fish."

"Dad, you've said that a thousand times, too. Will you please get off that crap?" I tell myself that as long as I paid for the boat and have Barrett captive, I'll keep on. Besides, for all his disclaimers, Captain Barrett seems rather to enjoy my going on in this way. It passes a day of not catching fish.

"But, you know," I say, "that's preliminary to more important things."

"Like what?" he asks.

"Like realizing it's you who's caught. You're caught trying to catch."

"That doesn't make any sense, Dad."

"Sure it does. Here you are out on a beautiful morning and you get all worked up getting these rooster tails tied on tight and placing these lines just right in the water. You tie yourself in knots yelling at me to keep the boat going at the right speed, and you're all frustrated because you catch only one Rainbow. Just think about it. Who's caught? You. You're hooked, man."

"Dad, keep the boat headed straight, will you?" Off to starboard lies an island the government set aside for Ospreys, one of the few places in the country where you can see these fine birds nesting. Earlier, when I called Barrett's attention to them, he didn't evince any interest in unusual birds.

"Maybe," I say, "what you really want is to be as free as the fish. You just don't know you want it. Or maybe you know, but have forgotten it. You need to be reminded. That's my job."

"That's crazy, too, Dad, that really is crazy."

"It seems crazy now, but when you learn the lessons fishing has to teach, you'll see what I'm talking about. You just wait."

"I can wait, Dad." I'm frustrated not to be making headway, but then I realize: I'm the one who is caught. I am caught trying to teach my son to be uncaught. Here I am talking to him about the lessons to be learned from fishing as though I, and not the fishing, can teach him what fishing has to teach. Better to be quiet and let fishing do the teaching.

It's like that job of his at Grand Lake Marina: whatever Barrett can learn from that job, he'll learn on his own, in his own way. I don't have to meddle. If I do, it'll do more harm than good.

Sybil is different. Her determination to teach our son exceeds mine. It's one of her gifts. She is further proof that, left completely to fathers, civilization would be going even more quickly into irreversible decline.

Sybil can stay after Barrett longer than I. "Hurry up, Barrett," she said one morning last week. "Barrett, you're going to be late for work. I've been telling you for two weeks you're going to be late, and you were. And, Barrett, you know what happened. Your boss called you in, didn't he?"

"Mom, will you please be quiet?" Barrett shouted. "It's my job, not yours."

Sybil spent the best part of the morning with her feelings hurt, wondering how we could have raised a son so insensitive, ungrateful, and rude, and blaming me for being an ineffectual, wimpy father, a charge I would never deny.

"Ted," she said, "you don't do anything when he talks like that. You saw he was going to be late but you didn't say anything."

"Was he late?" I asked.

"No, he wasn't late this time, but that doesn't matter. You've got to keep after him, or he won't have any respect for women."

"Frankly, Sybil, I don't see what any of this has to do with respecting women, but let me say it again: Barrett wasn't late."

"Well," she said, "he could have been."

"Sybil, I've told you that I think we ought to let Barrett handle that job by himself. My parents never told me how to do my first job."

"Ted, that was years ago and what your parents did is irrelevant, and you know it. And they should have talked to you more, anyway. And Barrett is different from you. You have to tell Barrett. He won't do anything if you don't tell him."

"He won't do anything if you do tell him," I replied. "He has to learn on his own. Learn to do by doing. That's the 4-H club slogan. My parents did teach me that."

"Ted, I don't care about the 4-H club slogan or the Boy Scout law," Sybil said. She paused to take a deep breath. A deep breath from Sybil is always a prelude to a new line of thought, especially when followed by a hard sounding "Teeddd." "Teeddd," she said, "if you don't teach him, he's going to end up without any values at all. He'll end up in the penitentiary, you wait and see."

"I can wait," I said. Deep down, I feared that she may be right. I am a wimpy, ineffectual father, and a disappointment as a husband, too.

With Barrett in the boat, I try again, but in a different way. This time, I'm determined to release myself from trying to teach him, just like he releases most of the fish he catches now. That's a good sign, I think, that he now can release a fish.

"You know what I sometimes think, Barrett?" I ask, now more in the mood to muse with him than to instruct.

"What's that, Dad?" he replies, paying scant attention to what I'm saying. That's good: you sometimes hear better when you're hardly paying attention, when you hear off to the side. Maybe I can sneak up on him.

"This is really going to sound crazy, Barrett, but, you know, I suspect that catching a fish sometimes does more harm than good."

"You're right, Dad, that's crazy, unless you're talking about harming the fish."

"No, I mean harming the fisherman. Take that fish you caught early this morning. What good did it do you? It only got you all stirred up to catch more fish. That's the only thing it did. Catching one fish overheated your mind and made you want to catch more. It made you think all the more that the point of fishing is to catch fish, when the point is something altogether different."

"So what's the point, Dad? Really, Dad, what's the point?" There is no chance of sneaking up on him now: all his defenses are at the ready. Maybe that woman back at the marina is right: you can't teach 'em anything.

But, then, maybe I'm not the teacher here, anyway. I can't possibly be the teacher. A guide maybe, but not the teacher. It's like fishing: there are no fishing teachers, only fishing guides. What has to be learned can only be learned by one who wants to know. Barrett doesn't yet want to know. He doesn't know that he doesn't know. He'll have to learn that first.

He hasn't the slightest interest in learning what fishing has to teach. Anyway, learning here is more like coming to an insight. You can't teach insight; it has to be realized. Insight has to dawn on a person in its own time and on its own terms. You can only point the way, and only to someone who is looking.

"The point is this, Barrett, the point of fishing is not to catch fish, but to change your self. When you throw out that rooster tail, you are throwing out a self that is caught: it is caught trying to catch. It's all frustrated and unhappy. What you want to do is to throw that self away. It's finally not a satisfying self, anyway. It can't be satisfied. And why not? Because it can never catch enough fish. Even if it caught all the fish in the lake it wouldn't be satisfied."

Barrett is listening now. Maybe he suspects I'm on to something. He must know I'm right: he wouldn't be satisfied if he caught every fish in Shadow Mountain Lake. It's always, "One more fish, Dad, one more."

"So, Barrett," I say, "you might try it sometimes: sometimes, fish so as not to catch fish. At least, fish without regard to whether you catch fish or not. If you don't catch any for a long enough time, you might be released from the frantic desire to catch fish. Then you'll enjoy fishing without catching fish. Then, if you do happen to catch a fish, you won't be overheated to catch more and more. You will release the fish and yourself. You'll be as free as a Rainbow in water."

He has no response for that onslaught, except to say, "Dad, that's crazy." Against the chugging of the Mercury, we settle into a long silence.

"Barrett," I say after a while, "why do you think they call this motor a Mercury? You know who Mercury is, don't you?"

"Of course, Dad. You think I'm stupid?" Maybe he is learning something at that expensive private school in Houston, but he doesn't have to be a smart-aleck about it.

"Then why call a boat motor Mercury?" I ask.

In a bored tone, he says, "Because the motor is supposed to be fast, like Mercury, only this one isn't. You think I'm stupid?"

"Ooohhh," I say. I've been coming at the question from another angle, and I forgot all about Mercury's speed. It's true, Mercury has wings on his heels. That's why he can carry all those flowers all over the place overnight. I was thinking only of Mercury as a trickster who carries messages. He teases and plays around with words and tricks people. To figure out Mercury's messages, you have to tease meaning out of words, and play around with words, too.

"But Barrett," I say, "Mercury is the god who carries messages. His speed only serves that. His speed is not important for itself. What about the messages? What's that got to do with a boat motor?"

"That's not for me, Dad. You're the one interested in messages, like what fishing has to teach. That's kind of a message, isn't it?"

"That's it, Barrett," I say, now encouraged with the way things are going. "They named this motor Mercury because they want the people who use it to think about messages."

"Dad," he says with a sigh, "you are out of it. Really, Dad, you're out it. You're full of it, too."

"No, Barrett," I say. "I think I'm right. That's what I've been talking about for the last fifteen minutes. Mercury uses fishing to give you and me a message, it's as simple as that. We just have to figure out what it is."

"Dad, let me tell you something: that motor is just a motor, and it is just like this boat, a piece of crap."

"Barrett, you know good and well the quality of the message has little to do with the quality of the messenger. A postman who is a bad person can bring you good mail, you know that."

"Dad, will you be quiet, please. I want to catch some fish. Anyway, the motor on this boat could just as well be an Evinrude. I know. I work at a marina, remember? We change out motors all the time. Evinrude, Johnson, Mercury, they're all the same to us. All we want is for them to get us there—fast."

He is right, and I know it: I am talking too much, and some of it is crazy. If I go on talking like this, I'll run out of words before I run out of life. That's probably what Barrett would prefer: that I go mute, the sooner the better.

Mercury chugs on, sending oil and gasoline fumes into the morning air. Over two-and-a-half hours we've been trolling, trailing lines of frustration in shadowy waters, with only one Rainbow in the well.

"Barrett," I say, "I think I'll write a book on fishing." This is a little game I play with Barrett to pass the time. I tell him about books I might write. Last week I told him I was going to write a book for parents of teenagers, and call it *Living with a Chronic Sleeper: A Guide for Parents of Teenagers*. It wasn't very funny, and Barrett let me know it.

"What will you call it, Dad? *How to Enjoy Not Catching Fish*?" His part in the game is to guess what I might call my book. Last week he said I should call my book for parents of teenagers, *The Glory Years*.

"That's a good one," I say, "but a fellow wrote a book called *The Tao of Physics*. That's Tao, spelled t-a-o, but pronounced 'Dow,' which is a Chinese notion that means something like 'way' or 'path.' I'll call my book *The Tao of Fishing*. I could use your suggestion as the subtitle: *The Tao of Fishing: How to Enjoy Not Catching Fish*."

"You do that, Dad," he says. "You're an expert on not catching fish. You might as well enjoy it."

Mercury carries us slowly back through the channel for the fifth time. At the top of a Lodge Pole pine along the shore sits a matted tangle of branches and twigs. The white head of a nesting Osprey rises from the center.

"Dad," Barrett says, "I think I'll write a book on fishing myself." It seems that now, for the first time, two can play this game as well as one.

"Oh, yeah?" I ask. "What will you call it? *The Frustrated Fisherman*?"

"That's pretty weak, Dad."

"Okay, what will you call it?"

"You remember the book that you gave me last summer, the one on tennis?"

"Yeah," I say.

"You remember the name of it? It's called *Playing Winning Tennis*. My book will be *Playing Winning Fishing*."

"Come on, man," I say," that's not what fishing is about."

"It is for me," Barrett replies. "It's just like me playing you in tennis. I want to beat you."

"But there are other reasons to play tennis, aren't there?"

"Sure there are," he says. "That book starts off talking about them. It says you can play for exercise and to be with friends and other crap like that."

"Like playing just to enjoy the game."

"That's for guys like you."

"What do you mean by *guys like me*?"

"I mean like what your friend in Austin calls you."

"You mean, John Smith?"

"Yeah, him. You remember how, when he sees you, the first thing he always says is, 'Estess, you old fart.'"

"So?"

"Playing tennis just to enjoy the game is for old farts like you and John Smith. Same as enjoying not catching fish. Only old farts would be interested."

I am stunned speechless. Something has gone wrong in my plan to guide my son into deeper insights about fishing. This couldn't be the message that Mercury wants us to tease out.

"My book," Barrett says, "is going to be for people like me. It's going to be for people who want to win."

"Barrett, you tell me, how do you win at fishing?"

"Simple. When I catch a fish, I win, the fish loses."

"Come on, man, be serious."

"I am serious, man. When I go fishing with you, I want to catch more fish than you catch. If I do, I beat you. And I want my fish to be bigger than yours, too. You see those guys over in that Bayliner? I want to catch more fish than they catch. I fish to win, man."

"That's crazy, man," and it occurs to me that I'm beginning to talk like my fifteen-year-old son.

"Dad, you know what, I bet my book will sell more copies than yours. I doubt *The Tao of Fishing* will catch on, no pun intended." No pun intended? My son is getting to be a real smart-aleck. When I get back to Houston, I'm going to take him out of that expensive private school.

It's clear, the woman at the marina is right: I can't teach him anything. There I go again, thinking I can teach him. I'm still caught trying to teach. Maybe I'm the one who is missing the message here. I've been wanting Barrett to learn lessons that fishing has to teach. But the lessons I want him to learn are my lessons, not his.

Perhaps he has already learned something from fishing, and he is trying to teach me. He has learned that it's fun to catch fish. If he is going to take the trouble to buy some rooster tails, rent a boat, and chug around a lake all morning, he had rather catch fish than not. I have to admit that that does make sense in an ordinary kind of way.

Barrett has learned that pleasure can come from the satisfaction of desire, while I've been pressing him to consider the wisdom that lies in its ablation. He and I are on different paths: his appears to be a lucid, single-minded way to satisfaction, which is to catch more and bigger fish. Mine is to remove the desire to catch fish, or if not to remove the desire altogether, at least to fish with a different attitude toward what will satisfy. I'm more interested in how he sees fishing than in his catching fish.

Nearing the marina, Barrett takes the wheel from me, commenting that since he now works at a marina he can dock a boat better than I can. There is no need to argue the point. While I gather our jackets and gear, he pulls the Mercury from the water, locks it in place, wets his hands, reaches into the well, and releases his Rainbow. He pauses for a moment to watch the Rainbow swim free into the dark waters of Shadow Mountain Lake.

"You fellas have a good time?" the woman at the counter asks.

I open my mouth to talk about our bad luck, but Barrett takes over to reply. "Yes, mam," he says, "my Dad and I had lots of fun. We really did."

"That's good, that's real good."

"Catch you later," he adds.

As we step into the bright light of mid-day, he puts out his hand and says, "Dad, give me the car keys, please."

CPSIA information can be obtained at www.ICGtesting.com
Printed in the USA
LVOW08s0855131214

418673LV00004B/403/P

## Catch and Release

In the afternoon Barrett and I drive up the gravel road at the south end of Granby Reservoir. After eight or ten miles, we park. Then we walk the half-mile trail up to Monarch Lake, which sits girdled by high mountains in northwestern Colorado. Straightaway Barrett gets a strike, and up out of the water leaps this Rainbow, a good two or three feet above the placid water of Monarch Lake.

"Dad, look. Did you see that?" Of course I saw that. What else do I have to do other than to stand and wait and watch?

"Dad, there he is again. Did you see him jump?" Indeed I did. We both saw curving out of the water, this lovely, glistening fish. In the air for a second, it reminded me of the falling star that I saw out of the corner of my eye last night, just for a second, out of the corner of my eye, a falling star dropping into the Never Summer Mountains.

By now the fish is swimming at Barrett's feet, straining at the line. "Dad, hand me the hemostats," he says. "I want to let him go." Fly fishermen use hemostats, the same as surgeons, to remove a fly without harming the fish. I am surprised by Barrett's request. I didn't know that he had a pair of hemostats. I am already anticipating squeezing lemon juice on this Rainbow at dinner, but nurse Ted does as instructed and hands over the instrument.

Barrett wets his hands before touching the fish: that keeps him from harming the sleek covering that protects the fish. I wonder where he learned that. Not from me, for sure. With the hemostats, he delicately lifts the fly from the lip of the fish. No damage done.

"There, little fella," he says. He cradles the Rainbow between his hands a few seconds to help him recover his balance. Then he unfolds them and lets him go.

I want to say, "Barrett, he's not so little. Let's keep him. He'll taste good off the grill tonight."

Ted L. Estess

"Take off, little fella," he says. Not realizing, I suppose, what has happened, the fish lingers a second, and then jerks to a start, as if to say, "Ooops. I'm free. I better get outta here." And away he scoots out of Barrett's hands and into the deep, as quick as a falling star.

It reminds me of that poem by Elizabeth Bishop called "The Fish." The speaker of the poem looks and looks at the tremendous fish that she has caught. At the end of the poem, she says,

. . . everything
was rainbow, rainbow, rainbow!
And I let the fish go.

Before we pack the gear and head for home, he releases seven Rainbows back into Monarch Lake. Each time I am a bit disgruntled. Seven Rainbows, each close to fifteen inches long, would be marvelous at dinner. We could invite the neighbors in for dinner. A little salad and a few glasses of Chardonnay and the mountain night would be pleasanter still.

This summer Barrett has become a different kind of fisherman. It's a higher order of activity, I suppose, being capable of letting the fish go. Surely, it is good, at least now and again, to be released both from the thing you have caught and from the thing you are trying to catch.

Catch.
Release.
You are free.